95

Dear Jerry,

– with best
wishes from
your daughter
and

Liv Ullman

1/21/85

ALSO BY LIV ULLMANN

CHANGING

CHOICES

LIV ULLMANN

CHOICES

ALFRED A. KNOPF

NEW YORK 1984

THIS IS A BORZOI BOOK

PUBLISHED BY ALFRED A. KNOPF, INC.

Copyright © 1984 by Liv Ullmann

All rights reserved under International and Pan-American Copyright Conventions. Published in the United States by Alfred A. Knopf, Inc., New York, and simultaneously in Canada by Random House of Canada Limited, Toronto. Distributed by Random House, Inc., New York.

Library of Congress Cataloging in Publication Data
Ullmann, Liv.
Choices.
1. Ullmann, Liv. 2. Actors—Norway—Biography.
I. Title.
PN2768.U4A325 1984   791.43'028'0924 [B]   84-47689
ISBN 0-394-53986-9

Manufactured in the United States of America

FIRST EDITION

ACKNOWLEDGMENTS

My greatest debts are to four women who in different ways made it possible for me to write *Choices*:

Marilyn Cain. I owe her so much for her never-ending warmth and support in my life.

Barbara Ball, for typing and retyping ever-new drafts and always giving creative encouragement, even in the midst of finishing her own book.

Kathy Hobson, who read through so many versions and never hesitated to offer generously of her time to lend advice and participate in fruitful discussions.

And finally, Linn, for giving me happiness.

I wish to thank Jean-Claude Carrière, who has left genial tracks of his learning throughout the book, and Peder Cappelen, for all his inspirational letters during the years of writing.

Furthermore, I owe thanks to David Outerbridge for his editorial comments, which were very helpful to me even when I did not always agree.

I could not have considered doing a book such as this one if I had not shared experiences and time with my friends and interpreters in the field from the United Nations Children's Fund and the International Rescue Committee.

A special thank-you to Bob Gottlieb, my publisher, editor, and friend, who trusted me to make my own choices.

Finally, thanks to Donald for reasons he knows.

And to Abel, who gave love.

THIS BOOK IS DEDICATED TO

LEO CHERNE,

THE CHAIRMAN OF THE INTERNATIONAL

RESCUE COMMITTEE, WHO INTRODUCED ME

TO IRC AND THUS OPENED THE DOOR

TO EVERYTHING THAT HAPPENED

TO ME AFTERWARD.

IT IS DEDICATED NOT ONLY

WITH ADMIRATION TO

A VERY GIFTED HUMAN BEING—

BUT EVEN MORE WITH LOVE

TO A DEAR FRIEND.

CONTENTS

PART ONE
CHANGING

D ECEMBER 31, 1982. I am spending a weekend in my cottage, which is situated on the edge of a cliff. Walking bundled up in wool against the wind, I stop to look at the ocean. It is the end of a year and my company is an old, beloved dog. The day is already losing its light, though we have only just passed lunchtime. Snow is covering the fir trees; the little pools of water in the granite are frozen into ice.

The dog and I have shared a meal. One big steak to each, meticulously prepared by me. Although my four-legged companion prefers her food raw, it was grilled today. Sometimes I like to do things for others in a way that pleases me.

The last day of the year, and my reality is solitude.

Down beneath me the ocean seems endless, stretching out dark and bottomless.

I walk along the cliff and my dog is happy, rushing back and forth, picking up sticks for me to throw. When I ignore her, she pauses momentarily, her head a little bent.

We walk on sloping gray stone that is slippery. I touch the weather-beaten trunks of trees we pass.

I bend over the cliff and look at the ocean.

The tides, the stirs and waves and storms of the sea. I have a vision of the myriad life and color and movement and danger under the black, uneven surface.

The sea is unchanged from the first time I walked these paths, drawn to the view of the water surrounding my home. It is changed only through what has happened to me.

I see the ocean as it is, but also how it was before. Within me lives the deep from that time undulating beneath the deep I imagine today.

In the almost-dark I watch the ebb tide leave the rocks glistening black and I decide to stay and wait for the emerging flood.

Time is my companion.

I am with the sea and its wide sounds and I lose myself in its rhythm.

The wind is blowing, sending chills through the dog, which despite her thick fur now wants to move on, jumping up and down to tempt me into following.

I smile and remember how I used to take all my toy animals to bed when I was small. And off we sailed to my daddy in heaven. What glorious journeys we had!

Sometimes I still carry a few of the animals up from their old, dusty, cardboard-box homes. I look at their glass eyes and torn ears, and I wonder if somewhere the little girl who was me can still be found attached to them as a smell, a memory of touch.

On a cold winter evening I remember hot chocolate and strawberry cake with thick homemade cream.

I remember playing musical chairs at birthday parties. What a lucky little girl I must have been, somehow always finding a chair to sit down on!

Those parties of my youth when the bottle kept spinning. Flashing in a dimly lit room surrounded by eager, blushing girls and boys. The kisses and the thrills and the encounters behind sofas and doors. And in dark corridors, awkward touches to be seen by no one else.

The wind is stronger, the waves have grown and are laced with white.

The dog has returned to our house, barking now and then to remind me that inside is pleasant. I am loath to go in.

My beloved refuge, a little place by the sea.

I look down over the cliff and can no longer see the sea.

The tide brings us what has been lost and wrecked and given to the deep. The spread of waves, their sound in the dark below me, comforting on this New Year's night.

I leave the edge of the cliff, the thunder of the sea, I bow my head to walk toward my cottage. The dog approaches me.

We are on our way to light the candles and heat the room to celebrate the beginning of a new year.

I know a woman who walked out a door. Ibsen's door.

I know what happened to one Nora after she left; she walked out and continued to let others make her choices.

Like many women in their forties, I grew up under a strict authority, where choices for the present as well as choices for the future were clearly understood to be choices already decided upon.

As a little girl I was told to be nice and quiet around grownups. I was taught to clean the dishes and the pots, and prepare the food. It was expected that I would become a pleasant wife, take care of my husband, have babies, and never divorce. Then suddenly, when I turned seventeen, women's liberation invaded my hometown. Now I was told that a real woman lives according to her own abilities. Thus everything I grew up believing to be true had to be questioned.

Whenever I felt liberated, one voice told me: "This is not for nice girls." But then when I was a good little girl another voice insisted: "A liberated woman does what *she* wants."

I had to listen to these voices in combat every day of my life before I could sort out what *I* really wanted.

Women of my generation fell between two epochs: before choice—and after choice.

But *after* choice there was a new set of rules, not necessarily tied to women's liberation, because after liberation from authority followed *pressure*: all the new ideas crashing in on women who were not sure how to direct their newfound independence. The liberated woman followed in the stream of others who, equally liberated, said what everybody else was saying, read what everybody else was reading. Conformed to that which everybody else conformed to.

Out of the new ideas grew the "free" woman who learned to understand everything about her own sexuality. She was told when and where to feel, when and how to state her own demands. And if ever she was confused, she bought another book, and searched for all the spots in her body where true identity was said to be hidden. And when she knew all there was to know about identity, she pursued the perfection of her own body, together with millions of other women privileged enough to have the time and money. Muscle tone and firm flesh became her new code words. When she failed in her diet she was overcome by a guilt worse than any she knew in the days before she was liberated. Depression over her body or occasional failure of confidence when the search for sexual fulfillment backfired overshadowed any other concerns that otherwise might have troubled her about the world she lived in.

For those who survived there was a new lesson to be learned: to conform for the sake of one's own tranquillity is fine, but not for the purpose of appeasing others.

. . .

Even as a survivor I didn't have the courage to make choices. I had a life with options but frequently I lived as if I had none. The sad result of my not having exercised my choices is that my memory of myself is not of the woman I believe I am.

Some things are unalterable: I am born. I am part of the tides of the sea. And in the end my wave, like all the others, will crash against the rocks. This is the inevitability.

But within this framework I have choices, and I am described by the way I make or neglect to make them.

I often wished I could start afresh, as a child again, and revive who I was *then* and who I wanted to *be*. I often wished to rediscover within me the girl who was innocent and full of knowledge before they taught me what life was all about.

In search of my lost innocence, I walked out a door. At the time I believed I was looking for a purpose, but I found instead the meaning of choice.

I did not know that when I walked out the door, part of my journey was already behind me.

I Remember Mama—a touching and humorous play—is being converted into a musical. The director tells me I am the only one in the world he could do it with. Richard Rodgers will compose the music. He says he can make me sing—I never did before. The producer tells me the role of Mama is a relief from the type of woman I usually portray, always in emotional trouble.

We make my choice.

I want to play a woman just coping with a normal life. I want to be a little lighter and hear some laughter. I am bored with the life of a tragedian, her rapes and her suicides, her neuroses and frigidity.

Each night in *Mama* I'll enjoy myself with all the others backstage. We'll sing and dance together. This should be fun!

On opening night I do a live interview for TV:

INTERVIEWER: Hello, hello and welcome.

ME: Thank you.

INTERVIEWER: Well, you went to Hollywood and were a fiasco there. How would you describe that?

ME: Maybe Hollywood and I did not fit each other.

INTERVIEWER: But you were *such* a fiasco in Hollywood. Do you know why?

ME: Not everyone can close down two studios within one year.

INTERVIEWER: Well, what's really happening in your career and life these days?

ME: I don't evaluate my life in terms of career.

INTERVIEWER: (laughs)

ME: I would like to say . . .

INTERVIEWER: (interrupting) Well, they say you're such a shy person, but you had a child out of wedlock and then you dated Henry Kissinger. How do you explain that?

ME: (pause)

INTERVIEWER: Well, it seems to be going better for you these days. Good night. Nice talking to you.

"Could you please sing a little tune?" Richard Rodgers asks politely. "It will make it so much easier for me when I compose your songs."

"I don't dare to."

"Sooner or later you will have to sing anyway," the old genius says mildly. "This is a musical."

"Oh, please wait—I am so ashamed of my voice."

"I have heard it all. Nothing would surprise me," he comforts me. "Don't be afraid. I just need to know your key. Sing anything. Sing 'Happy Birthday to You.'" The lovely man takes my hand and looks at me encouragingly.

I sing.

Before my eyes he ages twenty years.

At the beginning of our run, the theater critic of The New York Times was replaced. Since he gave I Remember Mama, my first and so far only theatrical musical, a terrible review, I contemplate sending him a telegram: WE ARE STILL RUNNING. WHAT'S NEW WITH YOU?

The show must take in at least $100,000 each week for the production to keep going, and the departing critic made that goal very difficult to achieve. Who wants to come and watch a star who looks "like a package of cornflakes when she smiles"?

However, the cornflakes star finds the critic's view of what is happening on the stage less disturbing than the preceding four months of rehearsals and previews.

New scenes, new songs and dances have been introduced almost daily. After the first few days of rehearsal, which I spend in a corridor just hoping there will be time to go through some of my scenes (the director is busy writing songs and auditioning children for another show he has running), I contemplate opening a pizza parlor or becoming an astronaut.

After five weeks I'm still an unrehearsed musical debutante already being displayed in previews before paying audiences.

A revised script, in hand as late as three o'clock in the afternoon, is given a trial run in front of 1,600 people the same evening.

The director is still auditioning actors for his other show. We will have two and a half more directors before opening night.

Fear is within the walls and nobody dares enter his dressing room after a performance because if the producer is sitting inside with a sad expression it means the actor whose chair he's sitting in will have to go.

During the three and a half months before we open on Broadway, twenty-two souls are disposed of, including three cats and two cat attendants.

We christen the stage entrance "The Revolving Door."

Every day some wastepaper basket contains sheaves of paper with my suggestions for improvements, which I scribble at night, unable to sleep. However, the director, who is also the lyricist, has little confidence in my suggestions, since I am merely a woman and a foreigner. He avoids me as best he can, even though this is a musical about Norwegian emigrants and I am the star. He ignores my lifelong experience with Scandanavian customs and, as it turns out, even wants me to change my accent.

His own Nordic knowledge turns up in the production in the most interesting ways. Mama is given a song about *lutefisk*, a Norweigian specialty of codfish steeped in a lye of potash. When I sing the lines, "Fish in a brandy, fish in a brandy, gently sort of souffléd," I always know when there are Norwegians in the audience, as their surprise is audible.

The older one gets in this profession, the more people there are with whom one would never work again.

Every Thursday, during the last act, a man enters the theater just to boo when I take my curtain call.

The first time it happens I am very upset and decide never to go on stage to curtsy again. Everyone realizes that this is nonsense, that I'm just being dramatic. I get no sympathy, although the producer does rush me flowers and champagne, standard medicine when a star is agitated.

For the rest of that week three people shout "Bravo!" from the back of the audience when I take my curtain call and curtsy.

We all wonder if the booer was paid, and if so, by whom. I wonder, when the bravos begin, if they too are paid for, and if so, by whom.

Nonetheless, even a paid "bravo" gives pleasure to a star so recently compared to a box of cornflakes; and on Thursday she smiles just a little sadly when the man shouts "Boooh."

I spend a couple of hours every day answering some of the hundreds of invitations, threats, charity solicitations, requests for autographs and engagements, gifts, flowers, and telegrams.

An elderly gentleman writes an indignant note to me personally: the two tickets he ordered had been sold to someone else by the box office when he came to pick them up. I write him a friendly response that it would be my pleasure to invite him and his friend to the theater on an evening convenient for him. Modestly I add that if he's still angry with us, it doesn't even have to be one of our performances.

He telephones my secretary and orders tickets to *Annie* for himself and five friends, and "All the way up front, please," because he is hard of hearing.

If a play runs for a long time, particularly a musical, some participants get bored and think up amusing little surprises to maintain the enthusiasm.

At the one-hundred-and-fiftieth performance of *Mama* a gigantic gorilla lopes into the wings just as I'm supposed to make my entrance. I fall on the floor with a scream of terror. Stagehands quickly pick me up and push me on stage. I am on Broadway singing "Every Day Comes Something Beautiful" and my body is frozen with fear, when I hear a discreet coughing in the wings. Out of the corner of my eye I see the propman take off his gorilla outfit.

An unknown man calls my secretary and asks her to arrange for him to meet me. She answers that, regrettably, I am so busy that I barely have time to meet my friends.

There is astonishment from the stranger on the phone: "But it's my understanding that she doesn't have any friends!"

I have a TV set in my dressing room and keep seeing myself advertising *Mama*, saying, "I grew up with Richard Rodgers' songs—and imagine! Now I am singing them on Broadway!" Then I smile, the way that was cute when I was eighteen. (They have asked me to avoid scaring away a potential audience with the "Bergman image.") The producer of the commercial wants me to remark that I received my first kiss to the accompaniment of one of Rodgers's tunes. My first kiss took place in the kitchen at home in Elgesetergate in Trondhjem when I was fourteen years old and in the background I could actually hear "Blue Moon" coming faintly from the radio. However, I was listening for the peal of bells my mama told me would sound when I met Mr. Right. The kisser had a ring with a big skull on it which he gave me.

Two days later my best friend told me he had touched her breasts to the same melody.

. . .

One evening Woody Allen is waiting outside the theater in his chauffeured limousine. He takes me to a preview of his latest comedy. There are only the two of us.

I am told not to laugh, even if I think the film is funny, because that will make him fearful when I don't laugh at something *he* considers funny. Then he lies down on the floor with his back to the screen and I chew on his house-keeper's chicken legs; afterward he drives me home. I invite him to see *Mama* if he promises he won't laugh.

He laughs.

Ingmar calls in the night and has read my reviews. He says they mean nothing: "More important for an actor is to bring a secret with him on stage," he says. "That's what captures the audience."

Easy for him to say, he who has moved to Germany with all his secrets.

Not so easy for me who doesn't dare look down at my feet when I'm dancing because a critic said that while I danced I was constantly counting the steps.

But Ingmar says that I should bring on happy secrets, and I try it the next evening.

Unfortunately, it is Thursday, and the "Boo Man" is there.

I am growing impatient. And bored. As an actress I like everything concerning the production I'm in to be mapped out before opening night. But how can I expect this from directors who trust that improvisations will cure the problems created by their inadequate homework? Six weeks after opening night I am still forced to improvise. I miss the directors I knew who would want moments to be *clear:* this scene is about *this,* and this scene is about *this*—and here the violin is playing, and here all the bassoons are playing. Good directors know all about that and will make it happen. *They* use the actors, they are challenged by the fantasy of whom they work with.

See me! Use me!

Just as in life.

I want to approach acting with the gift of my own self, my own experiences outside of the theater as well. In my dressing room, when the show is over, I sometimes sit and think of past productions—when I, on stage, lived in constant search of the character I portrayed. Never growing tired of her.

Oh, the wonder-filled evening when it all comes together.

When I am filled by a flow like a tidal wave and nothing can stop me. Nothing!

Oh, those wonder-filled evenings when I can act with passions, though not my own, but those I allow to pass through me.

When I can use all that I know about my own emotions.

When I can use my blush and my voice and my tears.

When it is my body moving.

But all belonging to another character.

Oh, those wonder-filled evenings when acting enables me for a short moment to have more life.

And then when I look back the next day it is the emotions of the character that I recall.

Her cry, her choking sound, her smile, the little step she took when worried.

The pleasure then of knowing I can sustain the way I felt for all the performances to come.

Sustain what I myself no longer feel, though it was *me*, in one of those evenings of wonder, who was briefly touched by a new awareness.

But for this musical, how can I use myself? I do not have the words or the movements to demonstrate what I know about my part, a peasant woman—the loving mama of a Norwegian emigrant family.

When I am not at the theater and not busy with all the social engagements that follow a Broadway star and not at home being a Norwegian mama in real life, I spend time with the man I love.

He is a highly regarded scientist, deeply involved in creating a machine that will eventually function like a human brain. Wires, computers, lights, pipes, and mice. He has several beautiful assistants.

He often reads poems to me, many of them he has written himself. He is very methodical—reprimanding me when he feels I am too impulsive: "You are not only the product of today, Liv, of this moment." I have told him I want to live in the "now." The sun is shining and I want to laugh with him and be like a child and for one day only have no past or future.

"You are the product of billions of moments from long before you were born. Liv, never forget that you are not without a past. It is in your history that you have your anchor."

I always feel weighed down when he says things like that. Though I write it all down when I'm by myself.

Most of our conversations, however, are about the brain. On our long walks we stop at small coffee shops. Sometimes, if it's cold, we drink hot red wine with cinnamon in it. I am very happy on these walks: the way his cheeks get color and his hair blows out of place. The way he walks—small and careful steps, almost on his toes, balancing the big frame of his body. The pleasure he exudes when he enters a shop and buys books and records for me, sharing what he loves the most. But always in the end we will talk about the brain.

"What do you believe will be the main preoccupation of science in the future?" I ask him one Sunday morning. It's too early for wine, so we're drinking chocolate with whipped cream.

He thinks for a while and then he says, with the light boyish voice that belies his fifty years: "I have no doubt that it will be the search for the correct definition of *error*. Error is the difference between a living organism and a computer brain. A difference that allows the capacity of the living organism to be able to make a mistake. Or, if you prefer, to get in touch with *chance*."

He pauses and wonders if I understand.

"You see, Liv, *hazard* does not exist in the logic of a machine. But it is thanks to *error* that we can learn something and never forget it and pass it on to someone else. Therefore error plays an absolutely necessary part in *survival*."

Whipped cream frames his beautifully shaped lips.

"Let us say you want to kill a mosquito. You have the perfect chemical product with which to do it, though you will find that *one* male mosquito out of a billion will resist. This mosquito will find from another billion mosquitoes a female who also survived. And together they will found a new race of insects that resists your perfect extermination product. The two mosquitoes, the survivors, compared to the other ones who died, were probably the errors, the monsters, of the group."

My lover studies me for a long time.

"Do you need the monsters?" I ask, placing my booted feet on top of his shoes to keep in touch.

He laughs and tells of a scientist friend of his who specialized in toads and frogs. "You should have seen him. He circled around his pond gazing at the jumping baby frogs, exclaiming, 'I'm looking for the monster among them!' "

He pauses and plays a little footsie with me.

"You see, Liv, what happens among insects happens among our cells as well. A monster will be among them, too. So this is what science in the future will explore: what is the *necessity* of the monster cell? What is it doing there?"

Long pause. He removes his feet from mine.

"A computer will always reject the monster, because it does not belong to the logic of the machine." He looks sad at this thought.

I am eager to demonstrate my knowledge: "But didn't Einstein say that God never plays dice? Didn't he say there is an order to everything?"

My lover stares at me and then says patiently, "He was wrong. Did you ever hear of Niels Bohr?"

I let my silence mean both yes and no—whatever makes him happy.

"He will teach you, if you could understand his writing,

that we are submitted to and depend on the *hazard.*" My
lover underlines that last word by lifting his cup of chocolate and swinging it slightly threateningly in front of me.

"The hazard is our master. The secret game between the
molecules." He starts looking for money to pay the bill and
I know he has an appointment and is going to leave me.
Hurriedly, grabbing my arm and rising from the table, he
says, "Science lacks the vocabulary for all this today. We
have no words to explain the secret movement of the molecules." Outside the coffee shop he signals for a taxi. "If science could give us a good definition of *error,* it would take
a giant step forward."

We are sitting in a wet car, because it's pouring outside
and the roof is leaking.

"Do we have a chance to survive an atomic explosion?"
Somehow I feel this belongs to the conversation. He looks
at me with satisfaction. I believe my best point with him is
to know when to ask the right question.

"No, Liv," he says. "No human life has a chance to survive in the form that we know it. Though maybe in a
monster form. Because some of the beings that we think
thoroughly different from us and useless, like bugs or cock-
roaches—*they* can survive any kind of nuclear explosion.
They couldn't care less."

And with this I am alone on the street in front of my
apartment building, watching my lover speed off to his lab
and his computer.

At least that was where he said he was going.

I watch the taxi disappear and I offer the empty space
after him this question: "If you had to choose between being

in a room with holes or in the open air when it rained—
what would be your choice?"

The taxi is gone.

I look sadly at the doorman, who doesn't seem surprised
that I'm standing in the rain addressing an empty street.

"It's more unpleasant and more humiliating to be in a
room with holes."

I flash the doorman my most charming smile and say as I
pass him, "That is, if you don't happen to like rain."

I have an old wok at my cottage.

I came with my lover and showed him the most beautiful place I know on earth. The cliffs—the fjords—the light—the lichen. He only saw the wok.

It is old and very rusty.

He laughed a little spitefully and said, "Why are you keeping that?"

I remembered who gave it to me once, who used to make the loveliest dishes in it. I remembered the smell of chicken and ginger. I remembered the sun outside. And I looked at my lover, who saw only the rust.

While he turned his back at me, I put my wok to work. Knowing it was going to be one of our last meals together.

My lover left me on a Thursday night.

Since he never finished working on the brain till after midnight, I went to dinner with a famous psychiatrist who wanted me to make a film for him. "I'll be showing only your face," he said, "and through your face we will learn about the agony of being human."

"No happiness?" I asked.

"Basically it is trauma. Your face is good for that." He patted my hand.

Then he talked of his mistress and told me about the lovely times they had together. I understood from his description of her that she would never have to personify agony and trauma through her face.

Just when I was about to say that I wanted to go home alone, he hailed two taxis.

Then I began waiting for the brain creator. Sometimes I wish he would be a little happier. On the other hand, if I insist on believing that it's spring and criticize a tree for having no buds, it's very unfair to the tree if it's still winter. So it's really all a question of seasons, or your idea of what season you're wandering in.

He finally phoned me at two o'clock in the morning from a telephone booth to tell me he wasn't coming. I told him I would have felt better if he had phoned me from the privacy of his home or laboratory, since he said he was working. "It's as if you rush out onto the street from something or someone who mustn't know about me. It's odd to be called up in the middle of the night from a telephone booth," I said neurotically, remembering his other calls from telephone booths. This made him so angry that he hung up, then called two hours later to tell me it was all over. "You are too difficult," his voice said, intermingled with music and people laughing.

It was already Friday morning and I knew I had one of those endless, bleak weekends in front of me. I looked into the mirror and saw this middle-aged woman who keeps invading my face. There was really more of her than usual. My perception of myself is not what I see in mirrors.

Slowly I recited one of his poems to the face that portrayed agony so well.

Maybe I never loved him. Maybe I just created him because I needed to. Maybe he was my "monster." I went to bed in the dawn and was awakened by a troubled thirteen-year-old girl. "Why does Daddy always call me 'little Linn'?"

"Oh, because we parents see not only your thirteen-year-old picture," I told her. "We see everything you were before as well. Other people see you as you are today, but to us you are also our memories of you, and in a few years our memories of this year of your life too. More and more the memories will look like who you finally are. Though you'll never be more final than today. Life will only add experience and change your body and your face."

"Do you always have to give such long answers?" she said, as she fell asleep in my bed.

And I thought of my scientist and his big, computer brain. And I shuddered when I remembered all the mice in their cages, running around, screaming; and maybe expressing pleasure as well. How do I know how it feels to be a mouse and have a human brain developed through experiments on my body? Already I am missing him less, remembering his machines and rodents.

And enough of these dinners discussing trauma in my face!

As a child I longed to be able to run over the dark water, enveloped by waves. And I wanted to explore the depths by swimming through the water till the bottom became as familiar as the surface with its billows and currents and small bubbles and white foam.

I used to wonder if I myself had once been an ocean animal. Why else would I long so for the abundancy of water?

Ladies of the sea.

Ladies of the sea—living in contradiction between dream and reality.

Acting out our quest for love.

Ladies from the sea—who represent feelings rather than ideas.

Ladies from the sea—our dealings with facts unfocused. And thus crippled where will and action would have served us well.

Our vision is the ocean—frightening, yet full of force—magnetic, too, for some of us.

Ladies of the sea: what *is* our choice?

Reality or hope?

Ladies of the sea.

In search of truth and understanding, we find in life that there is little room for dreams.

I was aware that there were refugees and hungry people. But they were numbers; statistics.

Never did I have an overwhelming feeling that they were my mother and my sister. That my grandmother was there, my child, and all the people I loved.

Toward the end of the run of our musical, I join other Broadway artists in a campaign to collect money for Cambodian refugees. We raise $200,000, which we decide to offer to the International Rescue Committee. When I present the check to the committee's chairman, Leo Cherne, I say politely: "If ever I can do something, call upon me."

He shows me some drawings by children of severed heads and people being stabbed. To the little Cambodian boys and girls these horrors of the Khmer Rouge were as common an occurrence as my daughter's getting dressed for school.

When *Mama* closes I travel to the border of Cambodia and to refugee camps in Hong Kong and Macao.

I see children facing horrors—hunger, exposure and disease. Many have lost their families and are alone.

I make this journey because I wonder whether I can use my status as a celebrity to raise questions, and maybe learn a few answers.

. . .

Walking at my side on the road to Cambodia are two men. One, who takes my hand, is a survivor of the gas chambers of Auschwitz, Elie Wiesel. The other is Aleksandr Ginzburg, a survivor of the Gulag Archipelago, his crippled feet stamping the dust.

Our trip has been announced as a march for survival. We are mourning the victims of Pol Pot's terror in Cambodia. We are protesting the invasion of Vietnam that followed. We want the people imprisoned behind the borders to know that we are aware of their plight. The world is not silent.

In front of me and behind me are hundreds of men and women walking in a long, narrow row, two or three abreast. I can see, when I turn, the abandoned peace of the Thai woods. And in the silence of the dusk, the quietness is disturbed by a bird frightened from its nest by the marchers.

As I continue on down the blistering and dusty road, I hear only the shuffling of hundreds of feet. There have been so many journeys, so many men and women protesting persecution and war and lack of choice. Men and women trying to express their grief and their despair.

Sometimes the world listens and sometimes the world understands. Often the world meets a demonstration like this one with indifference.

Though the marches continue, and in one way or another they somehow change the life of the traveler.

I walk on a dusty road in a futile attempt to enter Cambodia.

"We are among the last travelers," one of my companions says, "in a world where there is very little time left, where there is no longer a place for dreams, where the final act of aggression is on its way to release the travelers of the earth. To tell us we are no longer needed."

Our march includes leading doctors of France, labor leaders, business leaders, clergymen, bankers, lawyers, writers, intellectuals, and two performers: Joan Baez and myself.

Despite my fear of sharing a room with strangers, I find myself sleeping with twenty people in a tiny house on the border of Cambodia. With not enough mattresses for everyone, we have to sleep in shifts. In the morning we are woken up by bombshells. I wonder to myself what I am doing.

It has been a brutal decade for the people of Cambodia. First there was seven years of warfare, then three years under the savage Khmer Rouge regime.

The results of those ten years have been devastating for the country. Nearly all the skilled workers and intellectuals were put to death. Agriculture was disrupted, and the transportation system destroyed. Cities were forcibly emptied, and families broken up. When relief agencies first visited Cambodia, ninety percent of the children were malnourished. Thousands of citizens were fleeing to camps along the Thailand border. Those who survived faced disease and famine.

Over three million had already died.

Then Vietnam invaded Cambodia. It occurred during the harvest season, and Pol Pot's troops wantonly set fire to rice in the fields and to stocks already harvested.

We want to enter the country with twenty truckloads of food and medicine and fifty doctors who wish to stay there and give aid. The present regime threatens us with violent action if we cross the border. Forced to turn, we take our supplies to refugee camps in Thailand.

This journey changes my life. I am full of images that were never before part of my world.

I see children near death from acute malnutrition and disease. I see people too weak to walk the last hundred yards to food distribution points; sick people lying on the ground in a silence interrupted only by the coughs of those with tuberculosis.

I meet doctors and nurses who left secure careers to work here, many of them without pay. I watch the priests and the nuns who not only preach love, but who act in love.

I meet a twenty-year-old boy who one day, on an aimless drift around the world, saw a picture of a little baby, all skin and bones, and decided to go to Bangkok and see if he could be of help. Now he is off his dependency on drugs. He introduces me to a friend. She is a fourteen-year-old who came here with her parents, both doctors. At first she was told she was too young to do anything. Today she carries the old people who are too weak to move to the toilets, where she helps them and washes them before she carries them back.

An old lady rocking back and forth on her bed. All her belongings and two other people and their belongings are stacked close to her body on the same bed. This is her life: the little old lady who sits rocking on a bed in a foreign

land, without command of its language, left with a dream
of the day when everything will be different.

From Thailand I go to the island of Macao. Refugees
from Vietnam arrive in overloaded vessels, the boat people
who have not fallen victims to pirates on their journey to
freedom. Piracy is still flourishing in the South China Sea,
and those who are not killed often arrive raped and beaten
by the plunderers. They are terrified and speechless, survivors who have witnessed the slaughter of their families.
Many of the refugees on Macao refuse to walk on the shore,
to come close to water. Some refuse even to turn their heads
toward the ocean, refugees who were fishermen before.

There is piracy and thirst and hunger on the South China
Sea.

In the middle of the refugee camp is a shelter for lepers
who are tended by nuns in long gray dresses that rustle in
the heat.

Inside, I stop in front of an old, old woman lying in a
fetal position on her mattress.

Her thin, sorrowful moans are the only sound in the
room. For a long time I just stand staring at her, helpless,
my arms hanging at my sides. A passing nun gives me a
little pat on the shoulder and nods toward the woman with
no fingers and no toes and half of her face eaten away. I
slowly bend down.

Long arms envelop my woman, my grandmother, sweet
memory.

Gently I stroke her.

Carefully I rock her.

Gray hair in a long braid. Slender shoulders. Oh, Grandmother, I remember how your arms felt around me, the scent of your skin.

The moment I touch her, the old woman from Vietnam gives a little sigh of relief. The way crying babies do when lifted up and held. Sweet lady from far away, I feel great tenderness. Such a thin little body pressed close to mine.

After a long time of peace, I gently lay her back on the bed. She looks at me in fear and starts to sob again. A little wounded animal could cry like that.

A nun bends down, embraces her lovingly while telling me that always there is someone here with time to comfort and to hold.

An image of a frightened little woman fleeing in despair.

Monday morning, at the Hong Kong airport waiting to fly home, I write in my journal: "Thank you God for giving me this journey. I promise I will return the gift."

And Monday night on the plane: "I have just complained to the air hostess that the coffee tastes of chlorine."

DIED: Otto Frank, ninety-one, father of Anne Frank and sole survivor of the family whose two-year hideout from the Nazis in a Dutch attic during World War II was so poignantly recorded in his daughter's world-famous diary.

Only Otto Frank survived the family's concentration camp imprisonment.

I went on a long journey. And I came back awakened. A journey of discoveries.

I traveled to where the refugees live, and I am still traveling—traveling in a world of more than eighteen million refugees.

If I don't recognize them as individuals, how can I then comprehend the unbelievable numbers?

A frail and shivering old man who fearfully hides under his blanket when we enter his room: "Will something happen to me now?"

I walk out the door and it is as if I have seen the world for the first time.

This is Phorl's story. He is thirteen years old:

"I would like to go back and clean the temples. I miss them very much, just as I miss the mountains near our village. Of course I miss my parents, too, but I don't know whether I will find them when I go back. The temples and the mountains are sure to be there. But father and mother? I am not so sure."

A story with no name to it—since the letter was never finished:

". . . very painful treatment by Pol soldiers . . . forced my brothers and sisters and parents to work in their concentration camps . . . great massacre . . . great oppression . . . my soul lives helplessly alone . . . when Pol Pot was destroyed I returned to look for my family . . . just a few words that all the members of my family were killed . . . eight children, mother, father . . . oh, my God . . . just tears dropping down . . . I am alone. . . ."

To be made into a stranger. To live on soil in which one can put down no roots.

A loss that will never be replaced.

A little girl of about six in an enormous camp.

She is wearing my hat and carrying my bag, holding hard onto my hand, feeling proud that she alone from a big crowd of children is to have this special position with the grown-up visitor.

But suddenly she gives another child my hat and my bag and my hand, turns to a small boy crying, picks him up, and comforts him.

Her smile and her care for someone else even at a moment when she was the special one, her feeling of responsibility in the midst of her own privilege . . .

If you opened up my heart, you would find the sweet memory of children who are no longer strangers.

A little boy whispers: "Sometimes I cry, but only when it rains—so the other children won't see it."

The question is not: "Are we guilty for their plight?" Although the silent bystander is often as guilty as the offender.

But guilt is a prison for emotions, and stops the process of change and commitment.

The question is: *what* opportunity exists for those of us who witness misery?

For days a family huddles close on one hospital bed because Father is sick and they all want to be with him and share the pain.

Leo Tolstoy wrote: "I sit on a man's back, choking him and making him carry me, and yet assure myself and others that I am sorry for him and wish to lighten his load by all possible means except getting off his back."

It occurred to me that Columbus did not discover America, because America discovered him: he became Columbus only when a continent met him. And he met the continent.

A girl in a refugee camp discovered me. And I discovered her. She showed me what her life looked like.

Now I want to know more. I want to find out what life is to all of us, and how we use it, and whether there is joy in having it; and what we are for, and what friends are for, and why there are lonely people.

I want to discover the feeling of life as it begins.

I want to discover the feeling of life as it approaches its inevitable end.

I want to discover because we want to be discovered.

Otto Frank left behind his daughter's diary. It was only a few days before she was sent to the concentration camp that was to be her last stop in life that she wrote: "I believe that deep down inside, all human beings are good."

A field full of wildflowers, a heaven full of stars.

The breath from the former envelops me, the softest of scents makes me smile, while I turn my face upward. Quietly I make a wish: "Oh, let me love again. Let me be loved."

A falling star is said to grant one wish. But I made two.

People in my country, Norway, live close to nature. The sea and the mountains, the changing of the seasons, the light of the midnight sun, and the darkness of winter evenings. And as I am shaped by the elements, the elements in turn are defined by me.

I am filled with fairy tales, with trolls and elves and gnomes and legends. The fantasy of childhood stories invades my reality with passion.

When I was a child, a tree would be that wonderful blue dot with red and yellow things around it that I could paint. And only after grownups had told me many times that real trees did not look like my trees did I examine my dots and never paint like that again.

Fantasy, how I need it! How I miss my little boxes with their mixture of colors and the smell of paint and the sensation of making a thick red stroke on a big empty piece of paper.

And in the days of reality which I now live, I miss the glow of childhood when everything was possible.

I will call him Abel.

He came to me at a time in my life when I was ready to cross a valley on a rainbow, to live my fantasy of love, to believe in my dreams, and to whizz through the air with the birds, to abolish all borders.

It is early spring, and the first flowers poke out of their winter bed and stretch thin stems to the sun that's not yet warm. From the roof, small drops fall down from yesterday's rain. There is a touch of pink in the trunks of the trees, shining knots of birch with pale green at their tips. What a lovely day! People in couples along the road, and inside the houses, they light fires and I can smell the smoke.

From where I am, I see the ocean and a sprinkling of small islands. The light this April morning reminds me of the spring light in Norway when everything is reborn. I am far from home. We are making a film on the outskirts of London.

Just before I'm called in front of the camera, he approaches me.

I was expecting him and his crew the following day, to make a one-hour interview for Czechoslovakian television.

He is tall and very handsome. He doesn't smile, and says only his name when I greet him: "You are a day early."

After a while, during which we watch each other in silence, he tells me that he cannot do an interview without knowing me a little better, it is how he always works. He asks me if I'll have a drink with him that evening. Just for an hour.

Instead of saying no, I say yes.

My makeup man, who overhears us, smiles. I joke with him later and laugh: "You know, he might be the man of my life!"

He's already waiting for me when I enter the bar, although I'm ten minutes early. His white suit, the one he wore in the morning, has become wrinkly. I wonder if it's the only one he's brought. I see tenderness in his face and I want to tell him so. But I say nothing. Not then.

I notice that decisions are not his strong point as he ponders over the different possibilities of drinks as though his life depended on it. In the end, he orders whisky, and it turns out he never drinks anything else. When he speaks of his journey from Czechoslovakia to London, I feel as if he is the only person who has ever traveled. I detect an indulgence in pessimism in his character. I don't like that in him; but then, of course, on this first day it doesn't matter.

His hands are beautiful—large with long and strong fingers.

I tell him, when he asks if I live alone, that I have just reached the end of a long and difficult relationship. He laughs when I say that I need the illusion of protection.

"You are such a strong woman," he announces. I say that I wish someone would recognize my insecurity. I say that I am full of dreams. This he doesn't hear.

Just when I'm about to leave, he tells me he is fascinated by my face. He wants to touch it. He does. He tells me that he planned this interview at a time when he was long past being interested in listening to what other people were thinking. He was tired, indifferent, and disgusted. He tells me he had stopped believing in beauty and the meaning of words; that he used to sit in front of a new face every day and in the end not know what the face was saying. He didn't care. He couldn't even hear his own voice. He went on uttering words that were dead to him when he really felt like crying and when he felt like laughing, when he hated and when he loved. He became a celebrated slave of television.

He sits staring at his glass in a half-lit bar a long way from his own country with a woman who is a stranger. I believe he hopes that this woman will be the one who will relieve him of his loneliness.

He is still in his white suit the next day when we do the interview, and he takes off his watch and places it between us on the sofa where we sit. He wants to know about Ingmar Bergman.

I want him to know about me.

While relating an old love story, I think about the possibility of a new one.

While I am interviewed I say the words I have said a hundred times before. Most reporters ask the same questions.

I know he thinks *he* is making me say them. And I observe him, wondering if we will be lovers. Or if he will just leave with my voice on his tapes and my face on his film.

He is very self-assured, although later I will learn that this is a pose to hide tremendous shyness. It appears that he isn't interested in what I have to say, since he looks mostly at the ceiling while I talk. The evening before he had looked at me a lot of the time, laughing privately as if he knew some secret about me. Later I learn that this is how he expresses his isolation when drunk.

During the interview I tell him how Ingmar encouraged me and inspired me. How we inspired each other. I had never been so creative before him. I even wrote a film script because he suggested it, but when he read it he said it was too personal, that I knew nothing about dialogue. Thereafter Ingmar would watch me writing as if it was a cause of intense irritation to him. Even when the film script was buried in my desk I would catch him with that look.

To the stranger from Czechoslovakia I describe a relationship of long ago in which I lived within soft walls of sunlight and desire and happiness. To the man called Abel I smile and say: "Nothing can hurt me anymore."

Abel and I travel to a little village near Brest on the coast of France. The season is just changing from summer to autumn.

We spend a week together in an old cottage, painted blue many years ago by the owner, who rents it out a few months each year to tourists. It seems as though we were always part of this small house, experiencing the rhythm of the ocean we can watch from our window.

I have been in Brest once before—in spring. The seasons here are different from those I know so well in Norway. At home I watch green buds of spring turn into fragrant petals that for only two months fill my soul with joy before autumn colors the trees and the ground with a sense of departure. A golden beauty still hiding the winter, which, like a wild, cold animal, is waiting to pounce. Seasons I can never hold on to. Each one so short. Except the winter.

But now, with Abel, in a country where all changes are subtle, everything is easy to behold.

Only the ocean here shows drama. Sharing the tides with Abel, I become part of them. Their movements are ours, advancing and then retreating again, a cycle we can grasp and understand. The water rising, flooding the land, fish and seaweed and plankton in its midst. Nourishment. Then the sight when the water glides back:

Villagers who throng after it, both old and young. A mixture of sober and gay. We watch how some look for shells, stuffing them into coarse handmade baskets, to be sold in the market later in the day. The children catching small fish that have been left behind in little ponds and puddles. "There's our breakfast," Abel says and, holding my hand in his tight grasp, he pulls me along, running after the receding sea.

The sound—wasn't there a sound following just behind the water?

We watch in wonder at the way the profile of the landscape changes. The beauty of an early morning when the ocean, gliding over sand, softly, softly, leaves new paths on the beach. The glimmer of brooklets that will last only a short time, but, while they last, in constant movement.

Then the light, so special—the sun playing in water, and grains of sand creating their own piercing light. An old potmaker who captures this light in simple vases of gray, all very subdued since the light here is so strong that the colors are almost drained away.

Quick gulls try to snatch tiny sand clams, which reach up their necks to suck some water before it disappears again, then hurriedly, with luck, dig themselves down to safety.

The ebb offers us all kinds of delicious shellfish. A morning meal of oysters. Abel carries a knife in one pocket and some lemons in the other. I carry white wine. We sit on the dunes, eating while we watch a fisherman paint his boat in glorious colors. We listen to the sounds of the seashore, until we hear the whistling of the changing tide.

The fishing boats, which just a while ago were resting on dry land, are floating—rising with the power of the water. Our gray-white beach has disappeared, and now the sounds are great and wide. The fishermen run to their boats and hurriedly set sail; to return to their anchorage safely they have to be back before the tides change.

The seaweed, so pale and lifeless a while ago, is brought new color by the flow, while little fish and shells cling to its leaves like jewels.

Each day we see this miracle: how our beach lies there naked—accessible to all. And then the spread of waves drowning everything we have seen and touched.

We are both affected by the enormous forces of nature. One day I see a sea rose blossom just as the water returns. It is like spring. Yet on the day we leave, I wonder if it's been the tides that moved me most, not he.

For her thirteenth birthday Linn's godfather, Arthur, gives her two tickets for an African safari. His one condition is that I be the other traveler.

I hesitate: I am involved in activities for Cambodian refugees, I have also been away making a film, and I want to stay home for a while. Furthermore, Abel has left his country and moved in with us in Norway. "I have burned all my bridges," he told me when he came.

But it is a special gift, something for Linn and me to remember, and off we go. I write to Arthur:

"There is no way of thanking you for what you have given Linn and me. Allowing us to share secrets and confidences we never seem to get around to at home. Long beautiful evenings after having wonderful things happen to us during the day. Tired but very happy, we lie in our beds at night, whispering like two small children."

It is true that we tell stories at night. But as for harmony and shared pleasure when one is thirteen and the other forty? No. Only in my dreams.

I wish to give her love, wanting her to feel safe. Knowing what her needs really are at moments when I only manage to show her my own fear.

I do not want her to be looking for things in her later life which I was not able to give her at the right time. I would like her to avoid the fruitless search for that which can only be found now.

Linn and I on a safari in Africa: a mother forty and a daughter thirteen, both facing changes in their lives. We fight and we make peace and then we fight again. In her view, there are few things I can do right at this moment.

What we say and sometimes scream to each other under the palm trees doesn't mean so very much. The words are not what we really feel.

Linn does not want me to think she is happy. She hates the whole trip, that is her message.

We have arrived in a world foreign to both of us. For a short time she allows me small glimpses of enthusiasm. Then she remembers she is not to feel good and looks full of resentment again.

Our breakfast table is situated under a dignified tree and fragments of its white flowers spill into our orange juice. Birds surround us, sit on our laps and on our shoulders and eat from our hands, their feathers a rainbow of colors. One bird falls in love with her, rests its head slightly against her warm neck, singing a little as if talking to itself. It is the voice of bliss.

This is when she laughs, the braces on her teeth completely forgotten. A sound of happiness and wonder fills the morning air.

Then she tells me she is bored and asks if there's a camel around that she can ride. She knows we have tickets to go on a jeep; when I remind her, she informs me that she didn't travel all the way to Africa to sit in a smelly car. She says I am old, old. I say she behaves like a baby. She walks away. Flutter, flutter, our sociable birds fly off in all directions.

I do not move, I sit heavily, watching her erect little body. Around the corner of the last tent it disappears. Flutter, flutter in my heart.

Child, do not look upon me with such eyes. I see in them that you are angry. That even if, just a short while ago, we were laughing together, I must have done something to displease you.

If only you knew that reaching forty is as hard as being your age. I know as little about all the different emotions that are invading me as you understand the changing within your body. Both of us will have to wait a few months or a few years to find out who we are going to be next. Nothing is clear and nothing is sure. But it's all going to happen. Your thin little body will bloom, and your wonderful black eyelashes will cast shadows on pink cheeks when you blush with your secrets; and my body will never again be as graceful and my movements as powerful and effortless as when I was innocent about them. Maybe I will even look at you and envy you and then be miserable with shame. I watch you now, leaning against a tree under the shimmer of white blossoms. You know nothing of the adventure that is ahead of you as you become a woman. Today you only suffer, unaware that all the time you are opening up like a rose.

I sit here in a foreign country—my arms crossed in front of my chest, still with so much unspent youth within me. Like you, I am full of doubt; like you, I want someone to understand my insecurity, though I cannot tolerate my own adolescence the way I can tolerate yours. I want recognition in much the same way you do.

And in the meantime, while we change and while we wait for change, you have to fight and show your anger to free yourself from me—who finds it hard to realize that the time is now approaching when I must give you up and let you go.

Change need not stunt us, as it should not threaten us. We are in constant movement. My child and I.

When she returns, I tell her I am going to send her to a boarding school. "I can't cope any longer," I say. That usually produces a great effect—more than anything she fears the regime of such an environment. She starts to cry and I'm devastated. What a horrible thing I'm doing! Sometimes when I feel powerless I use my knowledge of her fear. I tell her I didn't know what else to say. I ask her to forgive me.

Inside two women there are hurricanes. And even though it is still morning, our first in Africa, we fall asleep again in our tent, holding each other tightly.

In the afternoon, we drive into the jungle. Vegetation and myriads of creatures in constant struggle for existence, in intimate relationship with the dry and rainy seasons. The sounds are of our car—of wheels on dry sand and stones; of the wind, of a running stream we pass. Over our heads, the sun is burning.

We pass a young lioness with three little cubs, all of them tumbling around in yellow, burnt grass, completely ignoring the fascinated intruders. The male is nowhere to be seen. We are told he sometimes eats his children, and thus is only welcome during mating time.

"Like my father," Linn says.

I let it pass.

Later our driver steps out to check the rear wheels.

"Is that dangerous?"

Calmly: "Oh, yes. If there are lions close by, they'll attack."

"But there *are* lions close by."

"Oh, yes, then you may get a nice picture."

Back in the jeep again, he tells us of a couple he drove some months earlier. The wife went on taking pictures as her husband was being pounced on.

We pass a lonely, peaceful elephant by an almost dried-out river. It looks so sweet, playing with some branches, heavy dancing steps, trunk swaying slowly back and forth in harmony with the silence.

Further along, where the river widens, a leopard is quietly eating its kill. A small animal on the ground, we see its stiff little legs pointing to the sky, its body stopped in flight.

We pass crocodiles and hippopotami, hardly to be recognized in the muddy water. Strange heads approaching from the river as if comparing the scent of the water with the air above. The muddy bottom wins.

Abrupt movements behind bushes of animals we cannot see.

And the larger silence.

Both Linn and I are excited. We sense the freedom of the veldt and where we're driving, the excitement of animal breath and animals running for their lives, coarse grass, raw emptiness, and the strange and haunting existence of wilderness.

. . .

"Dear Abel. We have climbed Mount Kenya and left our names in a little box somewhere high up in the mountain. I am bringing a stone back to you. Looking at it now while I am writing this, I am overwhelmed by longing."

In the nakedness of the African night, nature is stripped down to its own reality of animals and wind and vegetation —all moving, all breathing.

These nights are no more silent than those we are used to, but the sounds have more of a physical presence. Even when we hear nothing, the silence is still alive, telling us that something is happening in the dark.

Outside our tent sits an old man covered in a green blanket. He is our guard. Inside we are whispering stories. I tell Linn how the earth was born:

"One day a fire came out of heaven, all the clouds became red. Oh, Linn, you should have seen that fire. God was there, too. He made the fire. And when he had frightened everybody who had been bad in heaven, he put out the flames. With rain. It rained and it rained for millions of years. And the rain all fell on a piece of heaven that had broken loose during the fire. This was the earth and now it was finally almost covered by oceans because of all the rain. And then, after new millions of years, a little animal dragged itself ashore and that was the beginning of you and me."

For a long time it is quiet in our tent. And then Linn's voice wonders in the dark:

"I think I remember when I lived in the ocean. It makes me sad."

. . .

Outside we hear the sound of the jungle. A lion is snort-
ing close by, an elephant gives out a howl, and everywhere
is the hissing of crickets.

I glance through the night that has invaded our tent
and I find shadows and flickers in all the black. Within my
soul another woman lives, much younger than myself. A
little girl, who is me, smiles to no one before she falls asleep.
And it is dark and it is night—and we are there.

Soft morning winds and a blissful feeling of peace; awakened with a cup of hot tea served by the old man in the
blanket. He smiles as if thrilled by the expectancy of a new
day.

A short distance from our tent a herd of elephants is
munching audibly, and a couple of zebras and one giraffe,
looking slightly out of place, are staring at us.

"Dear Uncle Arthur. Thank you so much for your present. The most fun was the Balloon Safari. The way we just
glided through the air in our basket, with all the animals
under us. And when the basket landed and we all fell on
top of each other, everybody laughed. My mother had champagne with some grownups for breakfast. Thank you from
Linn."

I smile today while writing this, remembering a tiny tent
in Africa. The high voices from within, in anger and in
laughter. The sweep of sunlit landscape. A little girl asleep,
her hand covering the braces that she thought so ugly. Braces
long since gone.

I look out of my window at its view of a Norwegian fjord. It is raining. The landscape is so very different from the one of our safari. I see the dunes and sense the tides and hear the birds and know the animals and feel everything that grows.

My earth.

Oh, look at the rainbow. It is its own journey and its own goal.

Outside there is a winter landscape illuminated by a fading light. Snow is fluttering down. It could be a magical moment. But in this landscape the lovers are strangers. For a long time they lived only for the discovery of beauty in each other; everything else in their lives was left in a state of rest. Now they are slowly waking up, and the time of rejecting and destroying what they discovered is upon them.

We had first recognized each other when nature was in its splendor. The meadows of his country where we walked together glowed with lavender and red and yellow. Everywhere I looked flowers swayed on long, thin stems in warm summer wind, and the surrounding trees made tiny sounds in their perfectly poised branches covered in golden leaves.

"Like bells," he said happily. It was the place of his childhood, and he showed me every little river, every waterfall, every lake he had visited as a boy.

What lovely scents and warm touches—sweet memories —we shared that first summer.

It was then that we went to Brest and during long nights wrapped in each other's arms he would tell me how different I was from every other woman he had known.

Through me he felt he was being given one more chance. He felt that finally he would feel reality, that we would have a lasting love.

"You touch what I longed for but have never dared to touch myself," he whispered. And then: "You make me fly. You and I shall fly together. That is our destiny."

And so he left his country and came to me.

For years before I met him I tried to be what I thought people expected from me, even when alone. I wanted to scream when I smiled. I wanted to run away when I was close. I wanted to be silent when I talked. And when I laughed and raised my glass to strangers at cocktail parties, I was full of anger. They told me I was so gentle. They said they were attracted to my harmony. In the world of illusions and flattery, where I spent so much of my time, there was little room for me.

And then I met him.

He sent me a telegram requesting an interview. I never answered. Then he sent a second telegram. I still didn't respond. He told me later that he got scared he was starting to lose me without even having touched me; he wondered what was wrong with his little telegrams. Then he wondered if I had understood that he wanted *me*, not an interview. The interview was only an excuse and a justification. He simply believed that the two of us should meet and be together. And he sent a third telegram. That was when I answered and said yes. And at that moment, he told me, he knew everything that would happen.

During the interview I hid that I was different from him. I did not let him know that I filled my days with programs.

That I lived with schedules and plans. Obligations gave me security.

For him, the interview was the beginning of his madness —or so he would say later. Against all considerations, realities, and obligations—a brief insanity—he left his family, his job, his country.

"That I think is called love," he would say over and over.

Like another man, who once built a home on an island at the exact place where he first told me of his love, Abel offered me a similar symbol of passion: a universe with no past, with room only for two.

He showed me this symbol and I welcomed it—believing I would experience love through *his* action.

He told me that he recognized in me a woman who was in search of one true commitment, and he believed that his feelings for me were enough to fill his life.

He did not know if he chose me, or I him, but he believed there was a choice involved.

And then, awake and sober, he saw the difference between us. He was bothered by my telephones, my letters, my carefully programmed hours. He claimed that the leisure of love had become a prize to be won from me. "You are a victim of your obligations," he said, and followed me around like a sleepwalker until we both got sick of it. He wanted me, but not what my life was before and separate from him. And then he chose silence. He no longer felt any satisfaction, since he wanted only me, not my past or my present. Only me in terms of him.

He said, "Take me." But he only desired my arms, my smile, my body, my attention, my love. He did not want all the rest.

He said, "Use me," but he meant something else. I will never really understand what.

In our secluded little world of love I was warmed by his tenderness, though I missed recognition of all that was me apart from him.

He came to me at a time of his life when he needed to escape, when he longed finally to be one with another person.

I believed I wanted that too, but at the same time I was already on my way out of the environment that had been mine for so many years.

Since he committed himself so totally, with no reservations, I thought he wanted everything that was my life.

And then, without daring to verbalize what I had anticipated, I watched him withdraw.

He felt such alienation from my life.

I did not understand then.

We are sitting in my apartment in Norway.

He looks bored and stares at the flames in the fireplace. I am trying to read but the words mean nothing to me. He drinks. I ache for him and for myself. It will take a miracle to make the healing.

While I wonder if it is love I feel for him, I ask, "Do you love me?"

"Yes," he answers.

And then we are both silent.

I watch this man who is so much a part of the past he tried to flee. I picture all the events he must have hidden from me, the faces and emotions that are components of him.

Keeping to himself with pain I shall not know.

I remember the day he came, the way he laughed, running toward me at the airport: "Use me."

Oh, Abel, what happened to us? How could you ever believe I could be everything you gave up for me?

What did I expect? In the beginning I was full of joy because you claimed that your arrival was a gift of love. I needed that. Then I panicked because there was a real world around me that no longer could exist just as an isolated haven for two lovers. I had too many responsibilities, people who depended on me. I was a mother and I wanted time with my daughter. For me, a home was more than a place where he and I could be alone. Abel wanted a dream. He wanted us to escape together.

For me that was too late.

I weep.

"Abel, I am alone."

"Sometimes I am afraid that you need me only as a confirmation that you can love and be loved." He wipes my eyes and holds me close. "I love you."

"You told me—'use me.' "

"I told you—'take me.' "

"Abel, why are you always so angry at me now?"

He says quietly, "I'm not. You and I, we live so impatiently, with such lack of understanding. You and I are dreamers, both wanting the impossible to happen.

"My hope is that, through you, I'll lose my past. I promise I won't leave you, unless I grow certain that we two shall never be like one. Without a past.

"Though *if* I leave, I'll never look back. I'll leave you with no regret. I'll dream no more, but I'll have no regrets."

We are both silent.

The woman's fear:

Listen to the story of Rabia, a very famous woman in the Arabic world. She lived in the Middle Ages and was considered a saint by most people; the saying was that Rabia "was worth a hundred men." And this saint of the Middle Ages traveled on a pilgrimage to Mecca.

Rabia—the beauty of the Arabic world, crawling all the way on one side of her body. The image of Rabia, on a journey that took her seven years.

But when she arrived before Mecca, she got her period. Weeping, ashamed, interpreting her flow as a sign from God, she abandoned her goal of visiting the sacred courtyard and decided to go back without even seeing the black Kaaba.

I travel in an unknown world of poverty and need and hope. It is the *patience* of the poor that strikes me most.

Though I always lived close to the people I meet now, their lives known to me, I went about my life without seeing them. As if I were living on an island with walls around it.

Representing the statistics, a hungry man holds out a furrowed hand. He is old and all alone, with toes coming out of torn shoes and eyes that peer after every passerby: "Please help." He is the time bomb that eventually will destroy us all. He is the unimaginable poverty that plagues more than half of the people in our world today.

I will always be in debt to the UNICEF organization—the United Nations Children's Fund. One day I was called to their main office in New York and asked to be their first female ambassador of goodwill.

I was caught quite unexpectedly. My task was to travel to underdeveloped countries in order to observe UNICEF-assisted projects for child welfare, to get in contact with deprived families and learn about the circumstances in which they lived.

Then, based on my observations, experiences, and understanding, to find a way in which I could espouse the cause of children and their needs.

On the first journey for UNICEF, Abel chooses to go with me. I am happy for us both at this decision, since he told me once that he only feels alive when he's traveling.

Our voyage begins in New York.

An old woman at the airport lifts her flute and gives herself a little nod. A slender, mournful tune escapes her instrument. We stand there watching a heap of woolen clothes and bare feet with infected wounds, blue eyes gazing into secrets we cannot guess at.

"You see," Abel says, "there are poor people everywhere. Why do we have to go all the way to Asia to look for them? Your trouble is that you always feel you have to run ahead of events in order to make things happen. You never wait. You didn't have to go with UNICEF the moment they asked you. You should have given it time. We could have made plans and gone on our own, later. Seen what *we* wanted to see. Made our own choices."

I have no answer to this, though I know I cannot sit still observing the world the way Abel does, until all the moments have passed. Until one just feels ill.

I had hoped we would find something together, and now that we are on our way to India and already at the airport I fear we are further apart than when our journey was agreed upon.

The airplane lifts and drifts through cotton clouds into an enormous light that fills me completely. How I love these masses of luminous billows—to rest in them high up in the sky. I wonder what people in history would have felt if they had had this experience. Jules Verne, who took such endless voyages on sea and on land—how would he like to be sitting up here now? Strapped in a seat belt, but with the force of gravity annulled. Or Michelangelo? In his mind he had already abolished any limitations set by man, his whole life a celebration of the possibilities of the spirit. Would the secrets of his inner journey have rebelled against the sound and speed and restrictions of our flight?

Far below lies the transatlantic cable, carrying messages from man to man via the bottom of the sea, though the ocean shows no sign of it. Nor are any of man's countless journeys from continent to continent recorded on its surface.

And the space through which we fly tonight will never retain a trace of two lovers who passed by in search of purpose.

Each day 40,000 children die from deprivation of food, water, and medicine. That means every other second
now
and now
and now
and . . .

The poor seldom benefit from the miracles of development.

We who benefit can wait, but children cannot:

Nights without a roof, days with an empty plate, weeks of misery, months of emotional suffering—if they survive at all, they carry the mark for life.

And so do we.

We might not be aware that we bear such a stigma, but I see it. I see it on myself, I see it when I walk down the streets of New York or Oslo.

I was never innocent. Lack of knowledge could never be my excuse for turning away. I read and I listen to the radio and watch TV.

I *knew*. I just didn't *want* to know.

The statistics have been there before me, as they are on this journey. And even if they remain an abstraction, the particular faces of the living and the dying whom I meet now weave for me a portrait of the family of man. The beauty of the portrait is its threads of trust.

THE   LIVING.   He is an old man. Once a soldier, he is now the health worker of his village. Carefully, he shepherds me along the narrow path to a cluster of small huts. While one hand rests on my shoulder, his other arm is around my waist as if to support me, an arm whose thin bones and long sinews stretch a tight skin of leather. Hardened by the sun and the wind-blown dust, his skin is telling a story of an age and of a life.

He introduces me to all the families that are his responsibility. A recent education through UNICEF enables him, as a "barefoot doctor," to diagnose the common illnesses of his village. Inside the worn bag he carries, there are medicines and basic instruments for healing.

His pride when he sits down with a patient, and the tenderness with which he treats a wound.

During our afternoon together, I witness the respect given this old man by villagers who elected one of their oldest members to receive an education for them all.

In Bangladesh, a small community is celebrating.

Surrounded by warm, green hills, the men and the women and the children are dancing around a shining pipe. Around and around they skip, holding hands. Overhead, the sun is burning, adding color to their movements. One of them dressed in green, another in a floating cloth of red —a kaleidoscope swirls before my eyes.

Women here have always had to carry barrels of water for miles from an impure source. Now in their midst stands a water pump.

Vibrant as a bowstring just after the arrow has left, a

lively man who installed the pump is about to demonstrate his new equipment. Through the training he received from UNICEF, he is able to go from village to village, giving the people water. He helps me up an old ladder and tells me to put my hand on the pipe's opening.

"Feel it," he laughs, "feel it. The water is coming!"

Through my skin, I sense a rumble and the pressure of escaping air and the force of water deep down in the ground. The miracle is happening!

Dozens of hands are now on the pipe, and suddenly water is bubbling out and spilling over into cups and pans that are held ready.

When I cry out in pleasure, the well driller grins and I glimpse his palm, dark and dry, gesturing in front of me. I see a big blue mark on it. His daily work, pressing pipes in dry earth all the way down to the place where clean water stirs, has left on him an image of hope.

It is also while staying in this village that a nine-year-old girl takes my hand. Sweet little elf of a girl with long black hair flying all around her face and shoulders. She is laughing, and in a high and eager voice, while dragging me along, she tells me, "I want to show you everything that is wonderful in my life. I want to show you my home and my family and everything that grows."

She lives in a house of mud. I bend my head and enter through the narrow opening. Inside, it's very dark and I'm unable to distinguish the people who share this home with her. But through their murmurs and their touches and their breaths close to mine, I feel surrounded by warmth.

THE DYING. A woman follows me, carrying a baby in her arms. She tugs at my sleeve and whispers, "Please take my child. I can find no food for him."

Her eyes are gates into despair.

It is hot, midafternoon in a very poor village in India. The air is dead in this quiet place. The people seem tragically isolated, as if they're yet to be discovered by the world, starving to death in the midst of abundance. A woman collapses in the heat. Eight months pregnant, her weak body gives up as she finds herself in premature labor. She delivers a frail and underweight son and dies a few hours later from a fatal hemorrhage. No drugs or medicine are available to relieve her last moments. Her infant is still alive when we pass through.

THE ABANDONED. Outside an orphanage, a girl of twelve waits, holding a bundle with her few belongings. "May I stay? I would like to learn to read as well." She stands on her behind. A train cut off her legs.

Next to her, by the gate, there is a crib where mothers can leave their babies, ring a bell, and disappear. In case they acted on impulse and have regrets, the nuns wait for half an hour before coming out to collect the new arrival.

Abandoned old men and women are also welcomed. A screaming baby is lifted from its crib and brought to a timid lady in her seventies. I watch two toothless smiles when the child is placed in her lap.

. . .

When I walk into the garden, I see a sixteen-year-old boy sleeping on the grass. They tell me he is seldom awake, and when he is, there is no difference. He is completely without movement, except that his eyes will open now and then. Life seems to have fled his body, though through his lips I see a tiny stirring of a sound that never emerges.

The littlest children, unbearably skinny, move me the most. Their thin, rasping cries cease when they are lifted up and held. Faces so sincere, little noses, soft mouths—heads resting on my breast. A memory of a sweet lady in Macao.

Trembling little lives with survival a stretched thin thread of hope.

When I leave the orphanage, my dress is wet from little babies.

We are flying over Sri Lanka.

"It is fate," Abel says. "People believe that here. Even when they suffer the most, they believe it's been determined by their fate. We must not try to change it."

I cannot accept that. Abel and I, all of our friends, we all, to a certain degree, boast that we can be masters of our own fates. How then can the poor have a chance, since, as a rule, fate is never in their hands? And why would Providence give us so much and people here nothing?

It is hard to put into words to Abel what I feel in these days of traveling through deprivation; how I experience the questions I am forced to raise over so many things I used to find important.

The woman who wants to give her child away to save it from starvation is *me*. If I do not acknowledge her in the little span of time we share on earth, how can I expect to be acknowledged myself?

I see that it is only in statistics that people die by the millions. Each person dies individually, in his own predicament. The way he lives.

I seek words to describe what I am discovering and what I still am searching for. Is it love or faith? Or both?

Or what? I do not know . . .

Abel grabs my arm eagerly: there!

"Look outside! What we see from up here will make us wiser than all our visits to various communities," he says, leaning toward the window. "I want you to feel the *spirit* of these countries. Only then will you understand. Look out there!"

"But I want you to feel the *people*."

We fly over coconut trees and rice fields and artificial lakes and tea plantations. Abel points out waterfalls and rivers and valleys. Everything is wonderfully green and ripe. He is as happy as I've seen him on this journey.

The sky is blue and serene. It is close to sunset. Beneath us, the landscape changes from ripeness to barren, burnt-out earth, from richness to poverty. "It seems to ebb and flow like some secret tide of nature," he says.

Our small plane bends to the evening wind, and while flying over warm hills and grazing animals, Abel suddenly imagines he will turn into a bird, his wings outstretched, gliding in great curves.

"I wish," he whispers, "I wish that all the people in Sri Lanka could be with us now and see what a lovely country they belong to."

He is silent.

How can Abel and I feel in our hearts such an ache for the world's loveliness? How, when little children we've just met have hearts that are aching with misery?

THE LIVING. Tiny, dirty boy on a ferry, making an attempt at pretending he is dusting our car. A hand reaching out. Old eyes look at us indifferently.

We put money in the child's palm, some coins—we don't even know their worth. He looks down, then up and down again. A laugh of surprise and joy almost to himself. And then he doesn't run away as others have done.

A tiny boy in Sri Lanka washes and wipes and works on our car; even the wheels are brushed. Lovely, laughing boy is already starting his second go-round, a beaming face looking in at us, when our ferry comes to a halt.

Spindly legs without shoes run in front of our car as if to guide us off the boat. His leaps would make a dancer proud.

We drive off the ferry and we wave to him.

And there he is—time and place forgotten, sharing his money with another little boy. He has no time to wave back.

A middle-aged woman in Calcutta lives among garbage cans. She has found nothing to build a shelter with, she says. Not much privacy on this street corner, but she claims she doesn't care. She is surely much younger than she looks, since her four children playing on the wet, dirty ground in front of her are all small.

"Does she mind the smell?"

She doesn't feel it anymore. Chances are good here to find something to eat. She's often surprised by what people throw away.

The odor from the debris of man, scattered everywhere around the family, is terrible. A dog is sniffing eagerly at our legs, then barking while it leaves as if it's discovered something suspicious that it can't be bothered dealing with.

The woman has collected four pieces of wood, which she guards seriously, hoping to find something during the day to cook. When it starts raining, she invites me to stay under her shawl. She lifts it carefully over our two heads while we sit silently and in friendship in the gutter.

> Right now a child's bones are being formed, his blood is being made, and his senses are being developed. To him we cannot answer "Tomorrow." His name is "Today."
>
> —*Gabriela Mistral*

A little girl is brought from the street to the orphanage, her tummy big with malnutrition, thin black hair scarcely covering her scalp. Little flimsy fingers eagerly exploring the folds of my dress, the length of my hair.

She seems to love my necklace and looks at me while she strikes it.

I take her fingers and momentarily she intertwines them with mine. I touch the ring with a red glass stone that she is wearing.

And the child suddenly takes it off and gives it to me with one of those smiles.

A month later I tell this story to a group of young people in Washington. Afterward a girl of thirteen hands me a beautiful ring with a silver heart. She asks me to find someone who has nothing of her own, asks me to give the ring and say it was a present from a friend.

I then tell these two stories to a meeting of Quakers in New York. Inspired by the two girls, they mount a campaign in which every participant is given a little ring. For the month they have the ring before passing it on to someone else, they are asked to remember the two girls, and to send money to a special fund for children in need, and also to pass on the story.

In this way, in a few months, a little girl in an orphanage in Asia built a fund of more than $25,000 for other children.

Abel and I. This is our second winter together.

Outside a whistling wind, throwing hard sleet against the windows, small devils tapping on our walls wanting to come in. The night surrounds us with chilling darkness.

We are still lovers, but observing us is like watching two people mostly unable to reach each other.

When we went to Asia, I wanted Abel to write about it. He told me: "I am trying to understand the space around me, and I think my life is too small and too short to look for it so far away as India. The only thing I know how to do is read—"

For days he will be silent, even giving up working on his book. I look at him, wanting to shake him, though I don't know how to express what I feel. I remember a passage from *Little Women*: "I am angry nearly every day of my life, Jo; but I have learned not to show it, and I still hope to learn not to feel it, though it may take me another forty years to do so."

He says: "I only feel safe when I'm reading. When I'm reading I know the map of every mood, of every face, of every event, and I have no need to talk."

He is seeking reality in his books as I used to seek contact in my acting. We're living together at a time in our lives when he, who is seeking refuge in the world of written words, can receive no understanding from me who is trying to leave that world behind.

I look at his bent neck, his hands folded awkwardly in his lap, and suddenly I'm overwhelmed by the image of his isolation. What a shame, my love, that the people we met will remember your silence but never know who you were, as you will never know them.

Abel rises. Slowly and drunkenly he stops at each of the many lamps and turns them on. For a while he stands by the window and looks into the winter night. The north wind is engulfing our house like a raving maniac. Being inside, I should feel warm and secure. I do not. There is something about his back turned toward me. As if it is crying out a message I don't understand.

After a while, he goes back to where he was sitting. For a long time there is silence.

"Please talk to me."

"What is there to talk about? Why must you always talk?"

"Can we go to sleep then?"

"Why do you always ask questions? Why do you always sit here with me, and whenever there's a silence you ask a question?"

An endless pause. I want to reach him. When we are close and use no words, we still can overcome our distances.

"I want to love you, Abel."

"I don't want to talk about love. Let's talk about waste. You are wasting your life. And mine. You are wasting our lives."

"It's very late. I'm tired."

"The queen is tired. She commands me to bed. The queen is sleepy. We must all obey her wishes."

I can no longer stay in this room. I am impotent and afraid. The terribleness of not being able to count on him.

Every message we send each other now seems to be one of despair.

I blow out the candles I had decorated our evening with earlier. Then I pour myself a hefty drink. He sits. For a while I stand looking at him and then I have to leave. "See me! Touch me!" Silent cries.

The closing ritual is easier to handle. I go to the bathroom, brush my teeth, wash my face, turn on the alarm, put the safety latch on the door, and finally pull out the telephone jack. I used to put the little machine in the refrigerator and leave it there to ring among the cucumbers and tomatoes. That was before Abel. He didn't find it amusing, so I stopped doing it.

Suddenly he stands in the doorway. Again his image overwhelms me with tenderness. He is all alone, and he has only me to comfort him.

I do nothing. I stay silent. After a long pause he says, "I am suffering."

I hold him. Sit down on the bed with him. Comfort him like a child. Rocking him in my arms.

"I am suffering," he says again, and sighs and stares above my head to the ceiling, his favorite spot to look at when talking with me.

I don't know what I feel. Not now. I just know that he needs me.

He sighs again—this time, like an old man. And then he says to the ceiling, "You know, I wanted to put a limit on the world, to think about only one thing until the end. You." I smile. It sounds so beautiful—all my dreams that *this* time it's forever, finding rest in the man I love.

At times I need our isolated island the same way he does.

"Oh, Abel, we must work for our relationship. For you and me."

He turns to me, smiles softly and strokes my chin.

"I don't believe in working for love. I believe in loving."

PART TWO

CHOICES

Conversations. Location: Oslo, Norway.

Wide shot—the camera does not pan.

(*She and He have finished breakfast.*)

HE: How many times is it now that you've left me to travel?

SHE: I don't know. Will you be here when I come back?

HE: Maybe.

SHE: My home is like a prison with your *maybes*. Tell me what you're going to do. Tell me how you're going to spend your days. Tell me if you're going back to your country. Please—no more maybes.

HE: Greetings to all the people in Ethiopia and tell them I'm on their side because they're suffering. Tell them also that I'm lost to their cause and that I'll never go there.

SHE: I'll give them your message.

HE: Tell them, finally, that you know people who consider geography to be a matter of philosophy. They'll understand this because geography is a matter of philosophy to them, too. There will always be hunger.

SHE: Can you think of anything else?

HE: Ask them what love is for. Ask them what life is for. When we meet again, you can tell me how they answered and I'll be the richer for it.

SHE: Is that all?

HE: That's all.

SHE: That's all.

(*Cut.*)

On a December day during the current war in Ethiopia, UNICEF is given the services of a helicopter by the Ministry of Defense. It is an old, rusty Russian machine and I'm afraid while flying in it because the petrol tanks are on the outside and in the Ogaden desert beneath us there are guerrillas who might take aim.

Our destination is a small town. The minister of the Ethiopian Rescue Committee, who accompanies me, reports that it was "liberated" from the Somalians only two weeks earlier. "You are the first European to step on this land and observe the situation," I am told.

Standing by the helicopter, I do not know how to comment on the ruins of a life I see before me. I look at a destroyed town that they tell me was once beautiful. I see people who have made homes from remnants of their clothes.

The huts of cloth seem small, even for a child, though in some of them more than ten people press together and every movement has to be in accordance with those of all the others, asleep or awake.

I learn that their camels and sheep were killed and eaten by the troops that passed by.

"Do you know," the minister says, "both the Russians and the Americans can see us now with their spy satellites. They can take detailed photos of any area they want to, even focus on the epaulets of the enemy generals."

I did not know.

If they are circling over us now they will see a little group

of people walking through a town in which the fighting
lasted two days.

I am told the stories of men and women and children
who were shot. Did the satellite observe the dead left on
the ground when the smoke had blown away and the shell-
ing and the sound of fire had died?

I have an image of a man lying with his rifle still grasped
in firing position. Was he as frightened of killing as of being
killed?

We walk among the ruins. An old and almost naked man
follows me. "Why is there no food? Why did you come to
see us without bringing food?"

When told that the designated rations for this area are
very small and scarcely enough for the surviving children,
he says, "But I'm hungry, too. I hurt!"

I want to tell him something cheerful, and point admiringly to the little woolen hat of many colors that he's wearing. He tears it off his head in anger, puts it in his mouth
and screams, "Do you think I can eat it?"

A woman holds her child up to me.

"I used to live like a queen. I had a husband and many
children. I had a garden of vegetables. We had animals and
there was always food. Then came the war. This child is
all I have left. Look at his hair—it's falling out. Look at his
eyes—he's already blind. Please tell the women in your
country about me. Please don't forget me."

The minister walking with me in the ruins of a liberated
town in the Ogaden desert says:

"Earlier, we never had this kind of war between Somalia and Ethiopia. We never had refugees. We had an open frontier between the two countries. Our people are nomads. When the grass was green in Somalia, they would go there, and when the grass was green in Ethiopia they would come here. This freedom of movement existed from time immemorial among the nomads."

Government officials in Somalia would subsequently tell me the same thing in almost the exact same wording: "These people are guilty of nothing. They are just victims of circumstance. Aid shouldn't be tied to a particular government or boundary but to the people who are in need."

We pass a very old lady holding a small heap of dried nuts in her lap. I sit down next to her and watch her give from her ration to a little baby boy. She looks up at me, and without a word she peels a nut and puts it in my mouth.

She is about my age, her hair is long and shiny, she's covered in a beautiful red-and-white-striped shawl. Her skin is like leather and her eyes are bright; she never blinks. She heard the noise of the helicopter and thought it was bringing provisions—she can't believe we've come empty-handed. In the end she sits down and says she's decided she will just stay there till another helicopter brings food.

"Does she know it can take days?"

"No, she doesn't. She will sit and wait. And then, like many others, she will give up. Meanwhile, thousands and thousands of other people will hear rumors of our visit and come here hoping it means something to eat."

"How often do you use the helicopter to bring in observers instead of bringing in food?"

"Infrequently. When we do, the observers from other countries walk around and express their sympathy. They're very nice, but we seldom hear from them again. We can't give up, though. We have to believe that the world is receiving the message about the suffering of our people."

As we are about to leave, the woman runs up to us, looks directly at me and says with great dignity: "I do not know what other women *have*. So maybe they do not know what I *lack*. Tell them I have nothing except this shawl. Maybe they will give help. Or I will slowly die. You must tell them that!"

Promises never save a human being in despair. But perhaps, if someone listens, the despair may lighten for a moment.

Since suffering confers no rights on its victims, we who witness are the ones responsible for restoring these lost rights.

If help arrives only after all the people are gone, when the sands have erased the little traces that prove people once lived here, it is my duty to say: man was here. And now he is gone because I failed him.

Listen to the story of the camel. The one who lives on the Horn of Africa. When the nomadic people move from one place to another, they put all their possessions— their furniture, their goods—on the camel.

They load on the mats that make the roofs of their huts, then the branches that make the hut structure, then the food containers, then the water jars, then milk, and then the infant child and the newborn camels, and sometimes the old people, the sick people.

When you approach a camel, if you don't go slowly, or if your jeep makes a noise, the camel loses control of itself and starts running away in a straight line without ever stopping. There is no possibility of stopping him. Not even his owner's calling him by name can stop him. And what happens is that when he runs, little by little all the things on his back fall off.

The water, the branches, the mats, and the children.

Everything falls off his back—the newborn camels, the old people, the sick people.

It is dangerous when the camel runs in fear.

The camel can't be totally tamed, and isn't very intelligent. It is a difficult animal that needs a lot of attention, and the people who handle one must have a very special attitude toward him. But, for the nomadic people, the camel is everything.

The camel leads man to a grazing place, but the bush does not permit the big animal to move easily. So man has to open a road for him. Man removes torn branches for him, defends him from wild beasts, cures him of disease.

Between camel and man there is a symbiosis. They help each other reciprocally.

Far up in the northwest of the Ogaden desert, a man is singing to his camel, telling him that they are the only living beings by the enormous, plainlike, salty lake where they are walking. There are not even mosquitoes or flies, because nothing else is able to survive here, only the man and his camel.

And he is singing to his animal, "My dear, you are the most lovely animal of this world.

"You are the only animal who can live in this place.

"You are not only a beautiful and bouncy camel, you are also full of courage.

"You are the king of all animals.

"Look over at the mountains.

"There is a lioness hiding.

"But you are not afraid of the lioness.

"She is afraid of you."

And while he is singing to his camel this way, he also makes up the response, imitating the voice of the camel: "Yes, yes, you are right, my friend."

It is a very long song, in which the man forever phrases compliments to his animal while they slowly walk along in a desert of stone.

And with all that the man sings to him, the camel is agreeing. A deep and husky voice. And now and then a high-pitched one.

A nomad and his camel, walking slowly side by side. And neither of them feels alone.

Surma is in Ethiopia, close to the Sudan border. There are no roads to Surma and it does not exist on the map. A nomadic population has lived here for centuries. During an endless season of drought they were discovered by the outside world only when they began to die. Then, in a clearing between dried trees, the gray stones of the desert were removed and an improvised airstrip was prepared. In the middle of nowhere.

The Angel of Mercy, as they call her, is a forty-year-old DC-3, a flying trophy bringing into this hunger-struck wasteland a little hope. Two tons of grain to be shared among thirteen provinces.

Surma is not only the one. There is Bume, Kelem, Bale, El Kere, Chereit, Doolo, Imi, Bulki, Gode, Kelafo, Werder, Degh Bur.

You will not find all these names on the map, and perhaps they will disappear without trace, together with the human beings living there.

Silent people sit on the ground in long lines, covered with gray dust, looking up at the sky, listening endlessly to the changing sounds of the wind. This might be the day the Angel of Mercy is coming.

We make a bumpy landing in the clearing. They tell me I am the first white woman to visit Surma. We will stay just long enough to dispense what food we carry.

Patient little three- and four-year-olds, receiving their small ration, walk slowly with the wooden bowl of grain that must provide for one entire family. Small children are the sole recipients of food today.

A group of females sings to catch our attention. Last time it worked—they got a share. Maybe it will work again.

I watch the women, often with a baby sucking at their empty breasts, often with another baby wrapped close on their backs. They will travel long hours to find any nuts or berries that might still be left, or dried branches to improve their shelter. And since there is severe drought, they will dig enormous water holes—deep, deep down in the hard ground, without tools—only to find brown, muddy, contaminated water. In the desert, you can see the empty craters going on for miles.

Suddenly a beautiful experience:

A woman talks to me and then decides to dress me as a bride. I never learn why. She braids my hair. I ask her, "Shall I have a bridegroom as well?"

And she answers, "He is on his way to you, on a white horse, I promise you."

I say to another woman, while she puts her shawl around my shoulder, "I have a girl her age," pointing to her daughter.

And she smiles, "No, it is not possible, you are too young."

I say, "But you and I, I'm sure, we're the same age."

But she doesn't believe that.

Then I say, "Well, maybe you worked harder in your life than I have." She pauses, looks at me, and then she smiles and says, "Oh, yes, I think that you did spend a lot of time on your behind."

A girl arrives; her face is painted yellow.

"Why are you painted? Why is that?"

"It is something that we do. We know it makes our skin tight."

"Like a mask? A facial mask?"

"Yes."

"Is it going to make you lovely?"

"Yes."

"Can I feel? Oh, yes, it's a facial mask."

"It can be white or yellow. It depends."

"What is it made of?"

"It's from roots of trees."

"It's a beauty mask!"

"It's supposed to stay for half a day, and then we take it off."

"We do the same."

Some children pull me away, and we all run around and play a long, long time, and when I can't run any longer, I say I have to leave.

The children shout, "Come back and play with us another day."

I say, "I am too old to fool around like this," and they laugh, saying "It doesn't matter. We're young enough for you."

And then it's time to go.

In my memory will be people sitting in long and silent rows, human beings waiting patiently in the gray dust for food that might not come today, and not tomorrow, and not the day to follow.

In my memory will be a group of women still singing,

still empty-handed, as our plane starts rolling down the narrow airstrip.

I watch Surma disappear. But then in my memory this reality and a strange new image will be mixed together: when the pilot of the plane says he will show me a flock of wild white horses.

Long before we reach the mountain plateau where they are, he says, "Soon you will see. Oh, soon you are going to see." And when we are closer: "Now very soon we will be there—very, very soon. On the left side you will see them. They are white and they are wild. And no one knows when they came there. Suddenly, one day, they appeared!"

The Angel of Mercy circles very low over a high, square plateau with no roads leading up to it, and then I see them: a herd of elegant white horses quietly eating grass. Slim, strong bodies in perfect harmony, belonging to each other and to another world. Not even reacting to the sound of our airplane.

"They are wild, they are wild!" the pilot whispers happily. "And no one knows where they came from!"

And the Angel of Mercy makes a new heavenly circle, flying close to the mountain, as if it were a helicopter, and there they are again.

Beautiful, slender white horses, grazing quietly in the green meadow. No one knows how and why they got to the top of this plateau. But they were there, untouchable.

Then we lose them.

I am told that the Angel of Mercy lacks spare parts. Aircraft, like people, have their time.

Although I am not told of it, I know that in a year's time

the people of Surma will still be looking up at the sky and still be listening endlessly to the changing sounds of the wind. On that day the Angel of Mercy will not come. Not on that day or any other day. Ever.

The time of angels will soon be over.

I see her standing lost in agony with a tiny baby in her arms.

The area of her camp is severely affected by drought. Her child is dying quietly of thirst.

In front of her—a water hole with thick, polluted water.

She has a choice: to let her only baby die from dehydration or to let him drink of poisoned water.

I watch her make the choice.

She bends, her hand is cupped and filled with mud; she lifts it slowly to her baby's mouth.

In Somalia two or three thousand new refugees cross the borders every day. They now outnumber the populations of many African states.

I am visiting a refugee camp that opened a month ago and already 75,000 people have sought refuge here. Every day hundreds of new people pour in.

The existence of a camp is marked by the absence of trees and bushes extending out from the area for kilometers. Here the people can find no more fuel with which to heat their food, and no more wood with which to build their shelters. The first waves of refugees took what was available and now the land is barren.

How meaningless to counsel boiling impure water if there is no fuel.

Families have put their few belongings in a circle around

the place where they have settled—as if some plates, a little barrel, and a pile of clothes will give protection. How does one avoid freezing at night when there is no roof and walls to shelter one's body?

Two days ago a young girl of fourteen started to give birth under a bush while her mother ran around her screaming in despair. Screaming in the desert for her daughter. The girl's torment had become her own.

And when the baby, a boy, was born, after twenty-four dramatic hours during which the young girl in her struggle nearly died, the older woman just went on screaming.

I never heard the sound, but those who found the three of them huddled together in a no man's land of desert told me of her howl. She simply could not stop. As if the sounds from deep within her had become a part of who she was.

The small family was brought to the refugee camp where I met them.

The young girl is lying with her son on the sand. Since this area serves as a hospital, she has been given a cover to shield her child and a doctor has sewn up her torn body. The father of the baby is fighting somewhere in Ethiopia. She has not heard from him for seven months, and does not know whether he is alive or dead.

Three generations of a little family on the sands of a refugee camp, who will soon be removed from the hospital area to make way for those who are more needy.

The women stand in small groups waiting for a place to settle down. They greet me with the words *"nabad gallio."* It is a phrase for peace.

Some of them tell of how their children were forced away from them by soldiers.

One woman cries because she lost five girls and one boy.

One woman cries because she had no one to lose and always was alone.

One woman came with empty hands and is afraid they will not give her any food or water because she has nothing to carry it in.

One woman stands on boiling desert sand with naked feet and says, "You who hear of our destiny, please help us."

It seems to me that many of the people I meet have hope, although I am not sure they know what their hope is. But I believe that when in such despair, hope is the only right one has.

A doctor asks me to follow him, saying there is an old lady I must meet. He says she came to the hospital complaining about pain in her back and pelvis. She could not walk. She was very seriously crippled.

On the way, I pass a man who angrily stamps his wooden leg in the dust; a bullet tore his own limb apart. He bangs on the wooden leg with his fist. Bangs and bangs. He is carrying a child on his back, and he shouts, "This is what I am left with. This is my life."

When I meet the old lady she seems to be all right; she is sitting properly and confidently on her blanket inside a tent. This is her story:

"I came here only with a piece of cloth around my hips. My husband and my son were killed. I saw it happen—but no one touched me. On my way, I found a stream of water, but after I lay down to drink and had no more thirst, I realized that I could bring nothing with me for my journey, since I had no utensils. When I fled my home I did not want the soldiers to see me running away. I was so grateful because they had not touched me, and so scared because I watched when they killed my family. I thought if I left my house empty-handed they would not know I was escaping to be a refugee on the other side of the border.

"I do not remember how long I traveled. In the town I left, many people had died, and from that day I was always afraid, and I forget many things."

Later, I ask the doctor if she ever talked about returning to her home. He tells me no. She did not even want to leave the hospital tent. Each time someone mentions the possibility, she lies down and complains that her legs cannot move.

The doctor says, "She wants to stay here and be treated and taken care of. And I will keep her as long as I stay."

It looks colorful in the sun: the children playing, the hospital tents of bright yellow, people and their belongings, the primitive shelters made by the women from bent bushes, and, on the white and brown earth, pieces of cloth and rags stitched together, fabrics in every tone. But if you walk the camp at around six in the morning, the air is chilly and you will see small, thin bodies shivering. Children are about to die because even blankets are a luxury here. Little children sleeping close—oh so close to each other. As if they only can find warmth in other bodies as weak and thin as their own.

I wonder what they dream.

. . .

During these days my anger grows. I *want* to be angry. Anger allows action, the possibilities of change. The choice to protest.

Why is it that I, like many other women, have been brought up to deny my right to express anger? Why is anger considered unfeminine and sexually unattractive? Why have I watched in silence when men fight passionately for what they claim to be right, while my expressions of what I believe in are classified as part of a "woman's movement," not to be taken seriously? I have been scorned for verbalizing a need for change, a change from the political language of men and the pride and machismo and insincerity of many of our leaders. Not only scorned, but also judged as aggressive and even frightening to men. Small wonder that so many women are afraid of presenting their beliefs exactly the way they feel them; are even frightened by their own feelings of anger.

While we watch, men vent their anger against those who disagree with them, claiming they are serving a higher social purpose. Leaving us with a brutal and competitive world.

I am angry. I am furious watching children suffer while I know that billions of dollars are going to the machinery of war and the science of destruction.

I am learning that if I just go on accepting the framework for life that others have given me, if I fail to make my own choices, the reason for my life will be missing. I will be unable to recognize that which I have the power to change.

I refuse to spend my life regretting the things I failed to do.

. . .

An old man with a long beard is resting on the desert sand, surrounded by his few belongings. "Never again to walk into my own house, it breaks my heart. You see, no matter what sort of life you are enjoying, even if this camp had enough water and food and camels—it would still never be home. I want to belong—even in some little way to be given a feeling of belonging."

As I walk through a group of shelters, a woman asks me, "Why don't you cover your head? Married women do that here."

I tell her, "I am not married."

"You mean to say that women like you who live in big cities can't find husbands?" She looks at me kindly, pondering, and then goes to whisper with some men standing close by. After a short discussion, the men approach me, and the oldest among them says: "We do not want to waste our time trying to find a husband for a woman who is already married. Are you sure you are not married?" Again, I admit my singleness.

"You can read and write?"

"Yes."

"What we are going to do is get all the men lined up, and then you can make your choice. Our only condition is that you have to teach the children how to read and write."

I say, "But I don't want to marry."

"Listen, you have a problem that has to be solved. And when we have solved your problem, you can help us solve some of ours."

I say, "I want to live alone."

"Where do you come from?"

"Norway."
"The men from Norway are not men."

A woman comes running toward us. I have been told she was severely burned by soldiers before she fled to the refugee camp. A man who saw her arriving says, "I remember how horrible she looked when she came. She looked as if she was already dead."

I can see how badly she must have been burned, because her face and her body are different colors. She starts kissing the doctor's hands and repeats over and over, "Thank you. God bless you."

The doctor asks, "How is your hair?" She removes the bandage and some of her scalp is bare and I see the scars. The woman's tears are streaming down her cheeks and her face has a beautiful expression. "You saved my life!"

And while the three of us sit down, and children gather around us listening eagerly to a language they don't understand, with open mouths and eyes that do not miss a detail, the doctor tells me her story.

She was preparing tea for her two boys, who were harvesting wood. A family of nomads for generations, they had settled down close to the road. The approaching army must have noticed the smoke, and when they came near they saw an old woman peacefully getting tea ready for a big fire while a few yards away her two sons were working.

When the boys saw the soldiers they ran away, but she was too old to run. Besides, she was living her life quietly, not harming anyone, not taking sides in any war. The soldiers, led by a captain, came slowly toward her, and while she was still smiling, about to offer them some tea, they caught her by the neck, pushed her into the fire, and held her there by stepping on her face. The captain stood over her while she was burning and a soldier poured the boiling water over her old legs. In vain she tried to escape the flames.

Then, on the opposite side of the road, guerrillas appeared. They saw the parked trucks and what was happening. Leaping toward the scene, shouting, they started to shoot.

One of the bullets hit the captain who was standing with his foot on the lady's face, and down he fell into the fire.

There was an exchange of gunfire. The two sons, who had reappeared, were killed. When the shooting finally stopped, only three guerrillas were left. They helped the woman out of the fire. She told them of a daughter living about one hundred kilometers away, and they brought her there.

While she was living with her daughter, the village was attacked. She escaped on a donkey, leaving behind the dead bodies of her last child and grandchildren. She crossed a border with her mutilated face and burnt body. She moved from camp to camp until one day she came here and found the doctor who gave her life again.

He had a good shelter built for her within hours, and operated on her many times.

I watch the old lady's beaming face, her body leaning against the doctor's body.

I learn a proverb that has traveled for generations across the borders: "God created the Horn of Africa in a desert. But out of the sand grew a people of flowers."

. . .

The day of my forty-second birthday, the governor of Mogadishu gives me a present of the national costume of his country. I hold this garment, representing years of tradition, and I see it is divided into several pieces of cloth.

The first piece is flung around my shoulder, and two elderly women are for half an hour fully occupied with wrapping my present around me. As women do when intimate, we giggle, and with hands and mime make contact.

Curious, I look into the tall, narrow mirror. In the dimness of the room, in early morning, my body, wrapped in heavy fabric, is changing form.

It is then that I really experience the influence that can emanate from a costume.

The costume prescribes my movements, my features, even my ideas. But I will not have to act in it. This is for me alone.

My dress and I are watching ourselves in a mirror with irregular glass.

And in this poorly lit room in Somalia, making friends with two women without benefit of words, I become assured of my identity.

I remember doing a musical on Broadway. How long ago it seems. One evening I was standing in the wings waiting for my cue. I looked down at my long, washed-out apron and suddenly realized that I had spent most of my grown-up life in someone else's clothes. For more than twenty-five years I had traveled around the world—different stages, different film studios, different locations, and different costumes.

Always pretending I was someone else.

From early morning till late evening, in dresses made for another woman whom I, through impersonations, had to become.

CONVERSATIONS. The old man sings from the Koran.

He says he wants to talk about the Holy Book. "The message of the Koran should be believed word for word. Many things might have changed since Mohammed, but not the Koran, although interpretations can be different. The words of God cannot be changed by anyone. Constitutions and other things made by man may change according to the times, and people may adjust them to their particular situation at that moment. But the words of God are set."

"How much time do you spend each day with your books and your prayers?"

"I read most of the day and the night. I am old. I need little sleep. In the academy, and in my leisure time, I do what I know best—I pray—I sing—I read. I am a cultural adviser of my country, I am a Somalian nationalist. I have written one famous poem, everybody knows it in Somalia. It is one of our great national songs."

"When did you write it?"

"In 1941. My song is for freedom and independence. I mobilize people, I urge them to take action and show them how to take over their own country. By themselves. I ask the foreigners to leave and let the people of Somalia be free. That is the main idea of my song."

And the old man sings, and his deep voice is extremely beautiful. His eyes are clear and blue as a child's and his wrinkled hands are folded. When the song is over he asks me to sit closer to him and, as if confiding to a friend, he says: "I was praying for God to unite the people in the world and to help them forget all their terrible problems so that there will be no aggression. So that people can live together, and solve their problems in peace and unity."

"Did you write many poems?"

"Yes. I made thirty-two."

"Can a wise man be asked his age?"

"I am seventy-six and maybe some more."

"How many wives do you have?"

"Four. And maybe some more."

"Is it right to have so many?"

"Yes, if you are able to maintain them. And I am, so I married others after my first."

"Is it better to have four?"

"It is better to have one. But if you're able to, you can marry another three."

"But what is the best?"

"One."

"But since two is a problem, and three is more of a problem, why do you have four problems?"

The old man smiles.

"How many children do you have?"

"Let me count. Ninety-six it should be, with the grandchildren. Thirty-six are my own."

"Thirty-six children! From four wives?"

"I have had about nine."

"You married nine?"

"Some of them died. At the moment I have only two."

"How old is your youngest child?"

"Eight months. One wife is also pregnant." He laughs a long time.

"How long has she been your wife?"

"About eight years."

"How old is she?"

"Twenty-five."

"Is she also the mother of the eight-month-old baby?"

"Yes."

"Will you marry any more?"

"I am ready to marry another one. Maybe ready to marry a girl from Europe."

He looks straight into my eyes and again he laughs.

One night the field officer for UNICEF, Mr. B., saw the carpenter who was working on the new school project putting white paint on the body of his child.

The child was three years old. Mr. B. asked him: "What are you doing painting this child? He will have a skin reaction. It's not good."

"I don't know. Look—there's a bird in the sky, and this bird has its eye on my child. And if I don't hide my child, put this white paint on him, he'll be sick, and then maybe he'll suffer."

Mr. B. told him: "Oh, that's a lot of stupidity. Don't believe in such nonsense. Don't do that."

The man said: "You tell me. I'll listen to you. I won't paint the child if you say so. Are you sure you're right?"

"Well, I think it's better that you don't do this. And don't believe in such things."

The following morning, someone was knocking at UNICEF's door. Mr. B. opened it and Mohammed was outside with the child.

The child was running a terribly high fever and trembling.

The man said, "You told me not to paint him. Now look at the state he's in."

Mr. B. didn't know what to do. He took the child in the jeep and rushed to the hospital, put the child in the doctor's arms, and the boy recovered.

"From that moment, twenty-five years ago," Mr. B. said, "I have never interfered with the beliefs of other people."

And then Mr. B., who has been in Somalia working for different aid organizations for more than thirty years, tells this story:

"You know, we had a project for the development of crafts, and one of them was pottery. We were very enthusiastic. There was a Mexican professor in charge of the project who asked me to buy new modern equipment—you know, potter's wheels.

"The people here already had experience in pottery. For centuries they had made containers for water out of clay. But they used to put the clay on a circular stone, and sitting on the floor, they moved the circular stone with their toes while they molded the clay into various forms.

"The European type of potter's wheels arrived, and we taught the people how to use them. They were very quick in learning, and on the final day of the course, they thanked us and said:

"We're very grateful. And when you leave, we'll put all your equipment in the corner of our huts and let it stay there. But when you have some important visitor from Mogadishu or from New York, we'll take them out and show that we can use them."

The wife of a European diplomat is seated next to me at a dinner in Djibouti: "There are no problems anymore, you know. Everyone is getting aid. Too much, I believe. They become spoiled. It's really boring to talk about."

I am flying over Djibouti in an open helicopter. Every time we make a turn, I think I'm going to fall out. I'm very scared sitting in the open air, protected only by a metallic roof. For some reason it brings back a memory from childhood of my toy animals, the soft carriers of safety to the innocent. I remember putting them to bed every evening, carefully tucking them in, however tired I was. And when I couldn't find one of them, I would lie awake worrying. Knowing the fear of being left alone at night. Feeling how cold the animal must be. Wondering if it thought it was no longer loved.

From where I sit, I see the basic image of drought: what I believed were roads, I slowly realize are rivers with no water.

Djibouti has a population of 303,000 people, swollen by an additional 30,000 refugees. Fifteen percent of the population is made up of displaced people, forced to leave their homes and live in camps because of the drought. Nine out of ten pregnant women have anemia. Only seven of twelve children are born alive. Sixty percent of the children are malnourished.

The foreign minister accompanying me says: "We have so many refugees and we are very poor. But we turn no man away."

Memories of tea parties when all my dolls and animals were dressed in beautiful clothes and gathered on my bed— a little cup to each, cakes and drinks made of air, conversations forgotten long ago. A party interrupted only when my mother opened the door and announced dinner. Sweet aroma of food and warmth from the living room.

When I left Somalia, someone told me, "When you say 'Djibouti,' nobody wants to go there. Maybe it's not the end of the world, but you can see it from there."

I have written the name *Djibouti* in my palm with green ink so that I will remember it.

A woman runs up to us when we land at Ali Sabieh, a refugee camp. She is angry and won't stop shouting. She wants us to bear witness to the world about life's unfairness. She does not ask who we are. She has no teeth, which makes her speech at times unclear, even when she calms down. Her eyes are blind and she points to them. I have no other answer except to kiss her cheek, which is wet from tears of frustration.

I walk through the camp. It is very hot and everything is covered in gray dust. People around us are dying of thirst.

A pregnant mother sighs and, as if the effort was too much, she sits down on the ground, swaying back and forth, arms around her baby: "She cannot take food and I get no help from the health center—they help only the strongest because they don't have enough medicine. I sleep all day now. What else is there to do?"

We leave, and from the air I watch the children grow smaller and smaller.

The heat has caused me to perspire so much that my hair is all wet. I look as if I'm crying and the name on my palm is washed away.

And if he ever wept
I know today while writing this
His tears have ceased, his pain has ended.
My heart is full.
The image of a little boy who grabbed my finger,
Who gave to me the sparks of understanding—
It makes me want to make those choices
That are for him and thus for me as well.

One day I stopped believing the words of Anne Frank: "Deep down inside, all human beings are good."

One day I came into my hotel suite in Nairobi and the radio was playing "Jingle Bells." It was just before Christmas. The room was sheltered and lovely, and happy memories from childhood floated back to me with the music.

Then, from one moment to the next, I stopped *believing*, when the picture of a little boy in Somalia came alive behind my closed eyes.

An image of a child invaded my soul and my heart. A little boy who grabbed my finger and aimlessly led me around in a refugee camp. A little naked boy with an empty plate and eyes—oh—a hundred years old, and a tiny behind as wrinkled as an old man's.

I had to travel beyond my profession and the people I loved and the events I had known, before one day a little boy—an ultimate victim of war and indifference—proved you wrong, Anne Frank. A little boy showed me that we are not all really good deep down, because he was sacrificed to our lack of compassion.

And since then, this small child has been with me, and his thin little hand is still holding my finger. One small child whose short life was affected by those who did not even know of his existence. One small boy with no choice at all, because the choices were taken over his head and he was never even a part of choice. One little boy affected by cold choice, or maybe lack of choice, would very soon lie down on desert sand to die.

Thus I want to understand what *my* choices are and *act* upon them. Because choice is the essence of what I believe it is to be human.

I want to fight the forces that deny an individual or a people the availability of choice.

And since I understand that nothing is clear-cut, I must try to learn to accept the ambiguity as well, that life's most difficult moments are unclear, that mankind's most profound aspirations have costs as well as benefits.

The little boy who had no choice except living by ours.

I walked around with him, my finger clutched in his hand, my eyes on his little head of soft black hair covered with dust, a head that never moved or turned toward people we passed.

When I stopped crying for him, I knew he had taught me something, he had given me a perspective that deepened my life. Because I could no longer live with my innocence.

He forced me to live with choices neither he nor I knew about when we met.

I would like to dedicate my life to a child I never spoke to—who is almost certainly no longer alive in the desert of Africa, with his empty plate. And his wrinkly, tiny behind, and old, old eyes.

CONVERSATIONS. Location: Oslo, Norway.

(It is evening. The dinner table is beautifully set with shining silver and crystal. There are roses—an empty bottle of champagne. He is filling new glasses with red wine. She is carrying plates to the table—steaming, colorful food.)

HE *(tasting the wine)*: I hope you have written down your wonderful ideas on the hungry and the downtrodden. *(She looks at him. Passes the food.)*

HE: I must admit, your energy is more than a man could expect of a woman. *(Raising his glass)* I simply can't understand what such a lovely woman is searching for among beggars. But since I love you, I respect your choices. Welcome to where you belong. Welcome home. *(She says nothing. They drink. For a while, they eat in silence.)*

HE: Do you think some women are progressive because they are famous? *(She smiles. Says nothing.)*

HE: I have an important question. Have you ever asked where our money for aid to the hungry goes? *(She says nothing. They eat in silence.)*

(Camera slowly pans around the room where they sit. The books, the TV, the video player, the expensive hi-fi set, expensive furniture, some antiques, good paintings. Pause.)

HE: You look good. Traveling becomes you.

SHE: Thank you. *(Pause)* You look good, too. You've put on some weight. Being without me becomes you.

HE: I'm trying to look more like you. *(He laughs. Pause.)*

SHE: It feels safe being here. Knowing you spent time preparing this lovely dinner, that when we go to bed we won't be alone. (*She raises her glass. They drink to each other. Close on him.*)

HE: Why do you think you continually have to look for a purpose?

SHE: I believe we come to earth with sealed orders. I believe that only those who lack passion look down on purpose. (*She smiles. Pause. Cut to the whole dinner table.*)

HE: What is your opinion?

SHE: About what?

HE: About your journey.

SHE: Luckily, everything is very, very simple. (*She is silent. Close on him.*)

SHE: What is *your* opinion? (*Close on her.*)

HE: About what?

SHE: About everything. You're always asking *me*. You always comment on what *I* do. What *I* say. What *I* am. But I never know who you are outside of your books. (*Close on him.*)

HE: You have lost your vulnerability. And I miss it. You have lost your most feminine quality, my love. (*She smiles. And then she slowly rises from the table. She slowly folds her napkin. Slowly puts her chair in place. And then, in a split second, the smile vanishes and she screams. She crashes the wine bottle to the floor, thrusts her wineglass down, and runs out of the room. Cut to him alone. Cut to red wine covering more and more of the beautiful cloth. Fade out.*)

PART THREE

GHOSTS

This time my name is Jenny: "I wanted to live so that I never needed to feel shame as a woman and as an artist. Never do a thing which I doubted was right. I wanted to be honest and firm and good, and never have another human being's pain on my conscience."

I am making a Norwegian film. This long-standing commitment involves locations in three different European countries. Although it is good to work again with old friends from Norway, I find myself for nine months locked into many of the frustrations of my profession that I had hoped not to have to face again.

I travel and I travel. I pack and I unpack suitcases and bags. I wake up in strange hotel rooms. I go to work in different cities. I arrange to fly home to Linn. I wait for Abel at ever-new airports. I phone my lawyers and wire my agents, and answer my mail, and pay my bills, and long for Linn, and worry about love and count the days of separation. I am in action all the time.

It belies my statement: "The most important thing for me is to be a human being." What kind of a human being am I then, always tense and working? Always watching people, making observations from the life around me—as if, that way, I am really discovering something. Hoping to reveal a truth about some fundamental reality.

Am I a human being only through my work? Is there something I give in acting that I am unable to possess as a private person—allowing others, through me, to recognize what they have known before?

Is that Liv leading her human life?

Nora—I played the role on many different stages. I recognize so much of her. Is the theater my doll's house? Nora, Ibsen's lady who walked out the door. Nora, once a little girl in Norway. A little girl who paints her dreams until the grownups tell her she is wrong and show her how to duplicate on paper what *they* see: a reality that has no room for dreams.

My work should be the way I live. Thus my life is my work.

But roles do not change me; life does.

Too often, recently, I find what I am doing in the theater or in a film studio a cheat. It has become an effort just to move my feet from one side of the stage to the other. Laurence Olivier once told me he had a similar feeling when saying lines. It became a strain and he started to dread not remembering the next line while still saying the line before.

Maybe it is a midlife question. Maybe it has no name. Maybe it is simply awareness of choice.

·   ·   ·

Everything I experience lately moves me more profoundly, and my understanding no longer is limited by its early boundaries. I know less than before, but only because I am surrounded by many new questions and alternatives.

During this Norwegian film production, the need to leave acting for a while and make a change in my life is stronger than ever.

To step out of the stage door and be on my way. To turn a bend without knowing where the road will lead.

I do not want to arrive at the end of life and then be asked what I made of it and have to answer: "I acted."

I want to be able to say: "I loved and I was mystified. It was a joy sometimes, and I knew grief.

"And I would like to do it all again."

I am learning about compassion. I find its gesture in old people and in little children, in relationships and in solitude. I look for it in myself.

When most deprived, some show the ultimate compassion.

Long before I met Abel, I wrote a film script on commission. Then, surprisingly, I am asked to direct the film. It is only a fifteen-minute movie, one segment of a feature for which six women were each invited to write a version of Love. Can I direct what I have written? Dare I?

"Do it," Abel says.

"I have no time." Panic in my voice.

"I will help you," he promises.

Nonetheless, I am reluctant. It is risky, I feel, as I am used to interpreting drama a different way. However, I say yes.

At the last moment Abel withdraws his interest in my project. It is difficult for me to comprehend that our life together would be easier for him if I was less involved with events outside the two of us. Sometimes I believe that there would be less pain on his part if I actually failed. Like women before me and undoubtedly after, I am almost ready to inflict the pain of failure on myself to appease the relationship. Believing, wrongly, that I could thus make us both happier.

Loving me, for him, is a passion unrelated to my merits.

I am slowly learning that he loves me for reasons different from those for which I love him.

I take pleasure in his achievements, feel frustration when he does not move. Yet, deep inside, I am aware of the fact that I somehow expect *my* quest for purpose to be *his* as well; my movements to be duplicated by his. As if I have the right to ask from *him* an action to confirm *my* choices.

My film is about an elderly man. His wife lies senile in an institution. Old age, often so much more frightening and lonely than death itself. To endure decay and loss of awareness. Such a bitter end if you are not reached by compassion.

I want to tell a story of an old man who is the guardian of love.

I arrive at the studio in Toronto, hoping the work itself will actually teach me how to do it, reasoning that if I never try directing, I'll never know whether I can. While I pretend to be full of confidence, I feel that everyone is looking at me skeptically. However, Abel has urged me to give an appearance of great assurance when I'm working, even if I'm trembling inside; thus, even though there is hardly anything this first morning that I believe I can do, I convince myself that I'm in total control. Not so surprisingly, I learn that everything I've experienced technically in twenty-five years of acting points to the choices and the answers in this new capacity of filmmaking.

Very soon I start wishing I was in charge of the whole film, all segments of it, full of awe at all the possibilities a director has. I realize that I would miss filmmaking if I had to live without it, but only if, as now, I could make choices that are my own. A newfound ability to express firmness instead of politeness provides me with strength I never verbalized before.

"They'd better watch out," I say to Abel on the phone. "Now I'm going to take revenge for all the frustrations I've had as an actress, and make up for not being in charge all those years."

He tells me to hurry back to him. "And please, watch out! You're beginning to sound like one of those feminists."

The leading man, Charles Joliffe, is seventy and a lovely actor and person. He is a retired high school drama teacher, with a smile as sweet as a spring morning. His face is wrinkled and gray, with thin hair framing an open forehead. He exudes an innocence that we who watch have sudden urges to protect.

"I had to wait till old age for my first nude scene," he says happily, and stands stooped and naked, waiting to do his bath scene.

My film, called *Parting*, covers one morning of an old man's life.

He wakes up slowly in a double bed, his face slightly tinged by the rising sun, turning to the window with a soundless sigh. After a long while, he carefully puts his naked feet on the floor. In an enormous bathtub, only his small solemn head appears above the edge, the heat making pearls on his temple; soundlessly sitting there, lost in thought. Eating a breakfast of toast and tea—the kitchen table nicely set—while a cat jumps up on his lap, disturbing, for a moment, his solitude before it springs away when he reaches out to touch it.

A picnic basket is prepared with shaking hands: bouillon, carefully attended while cooking, is poured into a thermos, some of the fluid spilling out. Freshly squeezed orange juice goes into the basket, as well as a red-checked tablecloth, nicely folded. Finally, a bottle filled with water from the tap is added.

He walks around, locating this and that, while a change takes place. Anticipation becomes part of his movements and his expression: the old man has a secret. We watch it in his ritualistic preparation for a rendezvous. A face filled and lined by some emotion. Deep inside of him there is excitement.

Then we see him on the street, hear children's voices laughing in the distance. People rush past and no one looks at the slightly bent old man walking so quickly, as if full of important business. With determined steps, he enters the gates of a big, gray building. Proceeding down endless corridors, he stares at white-clothed nurses and doctors, daring them to delay him in any way. Finally, he stops in front of a door, its paint peeling off, and when he opens it—his *smile!* What a full smile! The expression of his face is that of a lover. An old man fills a dull hospital room with sunshine.

There She is!

A long time ago, his wife wandered into a dream. Since then, she has been lying calm and immovable, staring only at the wall in front of her. But now her knight is here, entering her castle with a basket filled with gifts, overwhelming the room with all the love they shared, creating tenderness around her bed.

Since there is no dialogue, hence no microphones, I can give directions while the camera rolls:

". . . Arrange her pillows, Charles. And now the napkin. Look at her hands, don't they look cold and uncomfortable? Now you start giving her the soup with the spoon you brought. . . . You're shaking Charles, aren't you? Spilling on her blanket. Oh, you're embarrassed . . . how difficult it is to age. . . . Feel it, look at her—your happiness, seeing how the food nourishes her. Do her cheeks blossom? . . . Try to make her take one more spoonful. . . . She doesn't want it. . . . She always was stubborn, wasn't she? . . ."

Watch the old man massage her quiet hands resting on the blanket. Look how he puts glasses on and brings forth their old, worn Bible. Listen as he finally speaks. In the profound darkness that envelops her day, his voice is utterly soft:

"Though I speak with the tongues of men and of angels, and have no love, I have become as sounding brass or a tinkling cymbal.

"And though I have the gift of prophecy, and understand all mysteries, and all knowledge; and though I have all faith, so that I could move mountains, and have not love, I am nothing.

"And though I bestow all my goods to feed the poor, and

though I give my body to be burned, and have no love, it profiteth me nothing."

On the windowsill stands a tiny potted plant. Carefully, he sprinkles it with water from the bottle he has brought.

His hand touches her face tenderly—oh so tenderly—healing her isolation.

The beauty of this hand that cares.

And then he leaves. Again, we see a little old man walking among people rushing by without seeing him.

He turns a corner and the street is left empty.

ME M O R Y .   My grandmother is sitting in an armchair. On her lap is a little girl, me. She sings. She talks about her childhood. She smells so good.

She tells me of a dog she loved that died, and how its death no longer awakens the pang of grief she used to feel. She tells me with regret that time will heal, will erase the hurt and sorrow.

I wonder why this makes her sad.

Soft hands caress two old and bony ones. And then my grandmother remembers a special day of spring, when she was fourteen and was running in a park with grass that was apple green. There were marguerites and one gorgeous yellow flower whose name she has forgotten. A blackbird silently flew up in front of her. It had been hiding in the grass. And she heard funny voices, a crow that tried to sing—and sometimes it succeeded. Ducks of different colors walked like drunken people by a pond. Close to a very lonely path she met a rabbit. And they talked.

I am sitting on her lap; it is very warm and safe. Embraced by aged arms, I see the beauty of another childhood so many years ago and the feel of it brings tears into my eyes.

I wonder why this makes me sad.

She kisses me and says that tears are pearls concealed in eyes. And like a miracle, when they appear, they set free everything that hurts far inside where all sorrow and all happiness exist together.

Later, in the dusk of evening, I am lying on a mattress on the floor, which has always been my bed when I am

there. In my corner of the room it is almost dark. My view
of her is framed by two small wooden chairs covered with a
spread. It feels to me as if I have a little house all to myself.

In this tranquillity I almost fall asleep.

The curved legs of the chairs form a cello-shaped opening, and through my cello I can see the whole room in perspective. At the far end of the window, now shaded by red
curtains, I see my grandmother undress, lit by a lamp with
flowers on its stand. It shines on her and on her golden
bedspread.

She lifts her woolen dress, and it is very painful because
her back is bad and her right arm crooked. She lifts another
dress of silk in faded rose revealing drawers, which are long
and colorless, and her stockings, which never fit neatly on
her legs. Her corset takes a long time to unhook.

Finally she stands there naked in the glow of light, and
she is sighing when she lifts away the bedspread. She never
looks at me, thinking I am fast asleep. Through my magic
cello I can see her, while my heart beats loudly with emotion. She does not hear.

Her braid comes loose with effort, and her hair is thin
and different on her stooped, pale back. A wrinkled body
is covered by a nightgown—a glimpse of a woman I have
never seen.

Another almost soundless sigh, longer than the first, when
she lies down. She turns with effort on her bed and sighs
again.

And never does she learn how she is loved in just that
moment when I see her hand reach out toward the light to
give the whole room darkness.

Our Doc, who art in
The Palais National for life,
Hallowed be thy name.
Thy will be done in
Port-au-Prince as it is
In Provinces.

Give us this day our
New Haiti and forgive not
The trespasses of those
Antipatriots who daily spit
Upon our country.

Lead them into temptation,
And, poisoned by their
Own venom, deliver them
To evil.

—A school prayer I am shown substituted for the
Lord's Prayer by President "Papa Doc" Duvalier
after he was excommunicated by the Vatican in
1961

I arrive in Port-au-Prince, capital of Haiti, on a Sunday morning. As far as I can see there are almost no other guests in my hotel. The manager runs to greet me with a big smile. He almost pushes me through the corridors and into my room while urging me to read a brochure that he throws at me:

> Lovely Haiti. Each day your pool will be cleaned and then sprinkled with fresh hibiscus blossoms. Each evening it is lighted underwater for a moon-light dip. And each day, compliments of the management, a bowl of tropical fruit in your refrigerator, and on your terrace we will serve you a delicious breakfast. In the night, dance beneath the stars, after you have dined from our world-famous buffet. Water-ski. Sail. Swim. Skin dive. Or just lie back and welcome the sun.
>
> Because that is what life is all about in wonderful Haiti.

I look around my ornately decorated room, with candelabra on the table by the bed. Green lizards are running over the whitewashed walls.

Just a block away, I find the reality of a different Haiti.

The streets are filled with garbage, beggars, vendors, and prostitutes. The poor people in the crevices of the city's center.

Only a few hundred wealthy residents have a sewage system, and in horror I watch the poor wash themselves in the leftover water coming from the mansions: men and women and children squatting by the sewer trying to be clean in others' waste.

If you have running water here and a swimming pool,

you pay around eight dollars a month for that luxury. While those who own nothing pay six cents for fifteen liters of contaminated water sold on the street.

The official minimum wage in the country is two dollars and seventy-five cents a day. But most of the poor I meet, if they earn anything at all, receive from a dollar to one and a half dollars per day. To place the two dollars and seventy-five cents minimum wage in perspective, one liter of milk represents one quarter of it, one dozen eggs one half, one pound of meat over one third.

Driving through the streets of Port-au-Prince, I see big banners displaying Papa Doc and Baby Doc "philosophy," specially and beautifully decorated with gold letters and many colors. Since illiteracy is very high, most people cannot read these messages, but when the president and his fleet of cars pass, the poor fall on their knees in worship.

Ninety percent of the workforce in the industrial sector is female. Women make less money than men and are not expected to organize themselves or go on strike.

There are no public latrines in the city. Only six trucks pick up garbage, and the waste is driven forty miles outside the city. But only if there is gas. Which isn't often.

In Port-au-Prince, two hundred human beings out of one thousand die from lack of food.

Mothers do not breastfeed their weak little babies. From what they regard as authority, they learn that milk substitute is better for the infants. Expensive powder, which they cannot afford, is mixed with unboiled, polluted water.

. . .

In the outskirts of the city, I see beautiful monuments to the dead. Grave after grave, like small ornamental castles. The custom here is that one must be buried in an elegant way: "Even though we have to live very poorly on earth, we want to live splendidly in death."

Two sisters share a tiny shack and invite me in. We seem to be the same age. The shyer of the two changes her shirt and puts on a cotton dress with blue flowers over her torn pants. She makes signs to her sister to do the same, but is ignored. I stand by the door, since there is nowhere to sit down, not even a blanket, but I feel welcome in this room without furniture. Once they had a bed, but since they never found a mattress, they used the bed for fuel: "We earn some money by cooking food for people in the area. It is cheaper for them than buying the fuel."

The sisters see my confusion and laugh: "You don't ordinarily think of eating out for poor people, do you?

"But if you can't find any charcoal or kerosene or wood, you still can get a piece of cooked food at our place for not so much money. Because we keep the fire burning for many families."

Outside their home, a mother is cleaning her baby, a boy and a girl are busy comparing hands, a man is quietly picking fleas from his dog.

The girl is just standing there. She seems to be around fifteen. Leaning heavily on primitive crutches, she is begging. Her left leg is terribly deformed, standing right out in the air, twisted—angling upward. Such a monument of deprivation. I am shaken in front of her. Her grief is so tangible—she just stands there silently in the midst of it.

The two sisters translate her story to me when she speaks:

"Once I begged a doctor please to cut off my leg. He asked if I had money and when I said I didn't he told me to go away. I can find no one who will relieve me of my leg."

The girl's lovely soft face is such a contrast to the crippled body, the deformed limb. Her voice is high and clear as water.

She never went to school. Never found any work. Does not think that she has family.

"Maybe if I didn't have this leg, my life would be better."

She has no shelter, no belongings. She does not know how old she is. She *does* know her name:

Charity.

In a flash I have an image of the old man in my film reading from the Bible to his wife. An echo—the words I chose for him to say a few months ago were these:

"When I was a child, I spoke as a child, I understood as a child, I thought as a child: but when I became a man, I put away childish things.

"For now we see through a glass, darkly; and then face to face: now I know in part; but then shall I know as also I am known.

"And now abideth faith, hope, charity, these three; but the greatest of these is charity."

It is afternoon and very warm. On the old veranda where we sit, only the mosquitoes seem to have energy, surrounding us with their monotonous sound.

Addressing me is a tall bony man in his late sixties, dressed very formally in a gray flannel suit, despite the heat. He is the self-appointed community leader of Fonds Parisiens, and men from the area are gathered around him:

"In 1947, when this whole place was a desert, our government decided to build a water system to irrigate the area. Thanks to the water, we were able to grow corn, beans, and other vegetables. Not only for ourselves, but for the communities around as well."

While he speaks the elderly man weighs each of his words. Noticing that I'm taking notes, he stops after each sentence and makes sure I've finished writing before making a sound of approval and going on.

"But in 1954 the hurricane Hazel destroyed our system—" He wipes his head. He is bothered by the heat but ignores the mosquitoes.

"The farmers never succeeded in repairing the water system because we had no equipment and no technical knowledge. Then we were granted a loan from the Haitian-German Agency for the provision of a water pump. Four years later a second pump was installed. Now we hoped to grow beans and tomatoes again. But we estimated that we needed to irrigate the earth five times after the vegetables had been planted, and the cost of irrigating was almost four dollars per hour, and the pumps started to break down. We couldn't carry out the repairs in our village, we had to get a technician to travel from the capital many miles away. And with the rising oil prices, irrigation became even more expensive."

For the first time he tries to slap a mosquito that has landed on his neck. He misses.

"Today we do not believe that we will be able to use the pumps." He takes a long pause. I realize that he wants the importance of what he is about to say to be introduced with silence. We share a moment of mourning the farmers' misfortune in life. Then he continues:

"The farmers here are very tired and don't know what to do. Ninety percent of us are Catholics, but we haven't been able to build our church. We can't celebrate the coming church holiday because we can't grow our beans."

The community leader of Fonds Parisiens rises slowly. He approaches me, stretches out a dry, wrinkly hand, holds my two hands for a short time while looking solemnly into my eyes. Then he goes back to his chair.

"I wish your visit here would solve our problem."

How do I explain that although one hurricane named Hazel could stop their growth, one accidental human visitor has little chance of making a difference in their lives?

He brings forth a little black book from his pocket and starts to read aloud from it. His voice is more somber than ever:

"In the years between 1954 and 1960 everybody had milk in the morning, red beans for lunch, porridge in the evening. Today, the richest can eat twice a day, though they are a few families only. The really poor, if they are lucky, can eat once a day. We never know from one day to the next if that will be the case."

I am sitting in the jeep, about to leave Fonds Parisiens. A young girl stands a little isolated from the crowd. When I turn and catch her eye, she very slowly and quietly points to her stomach.

I know that I cannot leave the car now and give her money. There are too many unhappy and disappointed people watching—waiting as she is. What do I do? What choice?

I turn away.

A very old lady in a refugee camp in Africa holding a small heap of dried nuts in her lap. I sit down next to her and watch her give from her ration to a little baby boy. She looks up at me, and without a word she peels a nut and puts it in my mouth.

During our tour of her Hospital for the Poor, she wants me to wear a smock over my dress. It is my last day in the country where her husband is President for Life.

My apron is yellow and very fancy. Hers is pink. This building is the cleanest I have seen in Haiti; the floors are sparkling. Every room is color-coordinated with the furniture and blankets. In the children's division, little dolls are waiting in each crib. Pictures of flowers and birds and butterflies on the walls. Lovely curtains matching the covers on the beds. The laboratories have the most modern technical equipment and there are beautiful, expensive operation facilities.

There are no patients here, however, except for a few babies. I ask her why.

The First Lady of Haiti:

"Unfortunately, we have not found the right cases yet."

Outside, five men pass me. Like horses they drag an enormous wagon loaded with wood. They are sweating and they look faint in the terrible heat.

Their best daily wage is one dollar.

In the remains of a tiny shack lives an old man. Over his door someone has painted: "The richness of a man is first his health and then his work."

If he could see, he would be able to admire the hospital I have just left, where uniformed nurses and doctors wait for the right cases. His bed is covered by a net and the woman who takes me to him says the neighbors want him to move away. The smell is bad and a black cloud of flies surrounds him. His head, grotesque in size, is partly covered by a cloth. I believe it is to shield him from the burning sun. Then the woman lifts the cloth and I see his face, all blue from what must be some kind of cancer. Worms are creeping through it, worms that she tries to wipe away each morning.

From a thin old body, still alive, I hear a frightened voice cry out for mercy.

I have been traveling a long time now, and I am determined to continue.

The different way strangers have touched my skin, all the new voices, those whose warm breath strokes my ear as I hear fragments of a life.

With my family and friends far away from me, I am never for one moment lonely. In a peculiar way, I may even be closer to them than when I come home and do not know how to communicate what I have experienced.

I find myself looking at pictures of children whose laughing faces, immortalized in a photo, are infinite reminders of trust. Women frozen in agitated speech or soft motion on my roll of film. Women who make me promise to remember.

I want to hold on to them, and I'm afraid that the normality of my life will drain their images away.

My grandmother tells me of a dog she loved that died, and how its death no longer awakens the pang of grief she used to feel. She tells me with regret that time will heal, will erase the hurt and sorrow.

I wonder why this makes her sad.

I do not want to slide back into all the old routines, and I turn down acting jobs, claiming to myself that I feel no motivation. Whereas the truth is that I am afraid to lose touch with the sense of reality and compassion that people I might never see again have awakened in me.

.   .   .

Only Linn is bridging the new experiences to my life at home. Her pains and her pleasures allow me, in a strange way, to hold on to my voyage as well. And when I look at her beautiful slender body moving here and moving there in eager anticipation of womanhood—her eyes, one moment sparkling, the next full of impatient tears, her sudden hugs and confessions, and her wonderful new spirit—when I watch all this, I realize that she too evokes homesickness in me.

I am homesick for my youth. Homesick for the days when everything was possible.

I travel not only for a purpose. I am looking for my lost childhood—the days when dreams and reality were interwoven.

I think of all the choices I never knew. And those I let be made for me—to please, from fear, for love. Where did they disappear to, those choices that I never made?

They are all part of who I am. They are the legacy I leave behind, they are the finished portrait of myself I cannot change.

I visit Auschwitz with a film crew. We are making a documentary on children who survived the Holocaust.

One of the women present was once a young child in this camp. Hannah is small, pretty, and very shy about detailing her experience of many years ago:

Silently, she watched her mother and father and her little brother forced away from her, and did not run after them. She saw her mother later, standing naked in a line to die. She says she did not cry.

When she was very little, her mother handed her a gift-wrapped dress of lovely velvet. "I love the color blue," her mother said, and held the summer-blue dress up in front of her.

On a sunny afternoon in Auschwitz, a camera and crew are following a little woman's path.

She walks from place to place and it is hard for me, the interviewer, to make her talk.

She steps into the crematorium with its big black ovens, and there is now a chill.

I put my sweater on; she does nothing. She stands in stillness, her head bowed down toward the floor of stone.

Later, when the camera and lights and crew have left, a lonely figure sitting on the grass, weeping soundlessly.

"You see, I also love the color blue the most."

In a noisy airplane on my way home, a memory of the small orphaned girl in Khao I Dang, the first refugee camp I ever visited. She walked for days after watching her parents murdered by Pol Pot in Cambodia. Finally, half dead when crossing the border, she reached this place. When I sat down next to her, she refused to speak. A little girl covered in dust in a camp where only the barest necessities of life exist. It is very hot. Suddenly, the child opens her mouth and a crystal clear voice rises in song to the sky—so full of longing. A child who hesitantly sneaks her hand in mine, while singing something her mother may once have taught her.

I am unpacking. Linn is there with me.

"Mama, I used to be afraid when you went on your travels, I often thought you would never come back. That you loved everyone more than me. But now when you go I understand it and sometimes I don't even miss you. One day I would like to go with you. Do you think I could?"

I have a memory from Linn's childhood:

On her father's sixtieth birthday, when his house was full of friends and relatives, the two of them walked down to the sea hand in hand. Her father asked her—she was only nine—what she would do when she was sixty. She thought a while and said, like him, a celebration, but only friends—no relatives. Though maybe she would want to ask her mother, who would come as a former actress, very old and silly in her conversation.

Her father looked at her and said: "But what about your father? You came to me when I was sixty. Won't you ask me, too, in fifty years?"

She turned to him and paused—and paused—and then she laughed, relieved, and said: "Oh, Papa! I'll have my party and when evening gets toward its end and everyone is dancing and drinking and eating, I'll take a walk all by myself down to the sea and there *you* will come dancing toward me on top of the waves."

. . .

Linn asks me: "Do you love Abel?"

"He used to make me happy. We laughed a lot together. Sometimes he would hurt me without knowing it. Now I'm mostly angry. He says he misses my vulnerability. He doesn't understand that I'm proud of my strength."

My daughter tells me, "I was once in love. He told me to eat only vegetables. And he took me for long walks. When we were alone he wanted to teach me about the world. But he never touched me. I wanted him so much to take my hand. He's twenty-two and he never calls me anymore. I think I loved him the most."

"When I was your age I used to spend hours with my girlfriend planning our whole life. We would share our dreams, wanting to do so much. But more than anything we fantasized about love."

"The first time I was in love you were so nice. He didn't want me. I was twelve years old and I felt so jilted. You told me you knew how much it hurt. And you gave me warm tea, and sat by my bedside.

"Once, when I was only twelve or thirteen, I sneaked up at night after you were asleep. I dressed in a long, beautiful dress. I put a lot of makeup on and wore a big hat with flowers on my head. And then I went out in the street. I love it so much, our street.

"And there were no people, and no cars—only the quiet, dark houses. And I ran up and down in the middle of the street, lifting my arms to the sky. In the end, I just lay down with my arms outstretched, and I had this wonderful freedom. No one was there to tell me what to do. I was all alone. That is my most beautiful memory."

. . .

She is sixteen.

I love her so. Watching her fills me with regret that who she is today will soon be gone. Remembered by me with such tenderness.

How do I explain time to her while she is still totally surrendering herself to a moment of sorrow or a glimpse of happiness?

Time is so different in her life from what it is in mine, where time is work and an acknowledgment of mortality. The urgency to celebrate before it is too late.

Time—photographs of people who once looked different, the shutter opening on mortality.

Time—all that came between me and what I was.

I want to ask her how the ocean smells and if she ever wishes to fly with the birds on her windowsill, if blueberries fill her with safety, and what she feels when the sky dresses in stars.

Not long ago she was still a child.

When Linn was two years old, her father came for one of his rare visits.

Out they went to walk in the deep snow.

It was very cold and she was dressed in her winter coat and her new warm boots.

Father and daughter walking in silence.

After a long time he sensed that the two-year-old was tired, and he lifted her up and carried her. Both of them looking ahead, one profile a miniature of the other, snow beating at their skin. Neither saying a word.

And so went the afternoon.

When dusk crept up on them, he heard her little voice for the first time. She was still sitting with a straight back on his arm, her face turned to the wind the way his was.

He heard: "My grandmother bought me brand-new boots."

And it was only then he realized what she had lost. He saw her naked, freezing feet.

A glimpse of two women three years ago in a tent in Kenya: one little woman looking down on breasts smaller than peas. The other woman watching and suddenly filled with a tender memory of times past when she hoped for miracles to happen during the night and that she would wake up in the morning with soft, round breasts.

Today, at sixteen, Linn is in full bloom. A woman has taken over the skinny body. The glow of her face is different, and the hair has a luster that is all new.

Yes, an element of envy is there today as I watch my child: once it was I, and now it is she with everything before her. How privileged she is, without knowing it. A tiny stab in my stomach, not wanting to deprive her of the right to have so much ahead of her, but wishing still—wishing it were me.

I am in the *middle* now, watching a small girl grow into a woman. It is enormously frightening and beautiful to see.

Sometimes I catch myself—or she does—trying to direct her into my path. Trying to save her from worries that were my own.

How do I imagine I can help anyone escape the hard corners of life? How can I believe that she and I will face the same life? How can I think that we will want to make similar resolutions?

Oh, look how the river proudly follows its own path. On its way to the sea tumbles the river of my childhood.

Oh, look how the water flows from its origin and even after going by returns as rainfall.

My grandmother tells me how everything travels.

One thing following another, everything is on a journey.

I am part of this motion—like the soil eroding from the dry mountains.

Flowing with the stream of water underground.

"Look at the flowers by the riverbed," the old lady tells me. "See how eagerly they drink, their roots washed by water."

The river of my childhood on its way to the ocean.

"It is sacred," my grandmother says.

And in the sunlight the stream rises toward the sky.

"It will return before sunrise to adorn the plants with dew.

"Oh, look at the motion we are all part of—the river and the trees and the flowers and the moss and even myself—we are all sacred.

"Look at the river following its own path," she whispers. "To interfere with it is to interfere with life."

"You have to act," Abel tells me. "What are you waiting for? Don't forget that your real profession is the theater. How will you ever function as a spokeswoman for your unnamed children if you just sit here and mourn them? You belong on the stage."

I am not so sure I do.

"Think of posterity."

"Posterity, frankly, has never done anything for me."

"What is it you want from your life, then?" Abel asks.

"Maybe to understand its purpose. Maybe to be free of ghosts of the past. Maybe to be in constant movement. Maybe, Abel, I am a Scandinavian oak tree."

He looks at me.

"You've never heard of them, Abel? They were growing far up in the north when it was still warm there. One day they somehow received the message that a change of climate was going to occur. And then they started traveling. From then on they produced their acorns on only one side of the tree—the south side—because that was the direction in which they were heading. Every tree, when it grew up, had its means of propagation facing south only. This way the Scandinavian oak trees traveled for millions of years until they finally settled down in Spain."

He smiles at me.

"So now you are a traveling oak tree? From what? Where to?"

"I don't know, Abel. Like them, I just somehow received a message."

As Mrs. Alving in Henrik Ibsen's *Ghosts* I am going to do a limited engagement at the Kennedy Center and, later, on Broadway.

Before this play was ever performed, Ibsen wrote to his friend Hegel: *"Ghosts* will probably cause alarm in some circles. If it doesn't do that, there would have been no need to write it."

I hope we can make a production at which an audience of 1982 will be alarmed as well.

A year earlier I get a telegram while in Norway, wondering if I will do Henrik Ibsen's *Ghosts*. That must be the English translation of *When We Dead Awaken*, almost my favorite Ibsen. I am exactly the right age for the leading character, Irene, and during all my years as an actress in the theater, I always wanted one day to portray her. A telegram goes back to the United States: "I would love to do *Ghosts*."

For half a year I read and prepare for Ibsen's lovely masterpiece on art and dreams and death. One day a friend asks me: "What do they call this play in English?"

"Ghosts."

"Ghosts? Oh, Liv—that's another play. That's Mrs. Alving's play."

I have said yes to doing a woman years older than my-

self. Finally the limitation of being a Norwegian dealing
with her work in English has hit me hard.

I am too embarrassed to back out.

Ghosts is a play about fears—a drama of people who
never dare to live by their choices, bound by the conformity
of conventions.

It is the drama of a young man, Osvald, longing for the
sunshine, free of shadows from the past; a boy who worships
the arts and Sundays and love but fears that the joy of life
will never be his, as the laws of order established by a stag-
nated society, "the ghosts," are in the process of suffocating
him.

I shall portray his mother, a well-read woman who, during her years of solitude, has grown most wise, though
never daring to verbalize what she has understood, hiding
behind lies instead. Creating ghosts while trying to expunge
them.

I believe I have both knowledge and experience that will
prove fruitful for this production.

Since the play is to get a new American adaptation, I am
asked to make a literal translation into English from the
Norwegian original. I spend most of December 1981 en-
grossed in this, enjoying the work tremendously.

Abel's book is progressing slowly. He will labor over a
single page for days, but when he sometimes reads to me
what he has written, I am very moved. He has such beautiful images, though they are full of pain. Maybe his pas-
sionate soul will always seek pain, will deny him the
possibility of happiness.

We work in the living room. One side of our big desk surrounded by sorrow—the other confronting ghosts.

Already within me, I feel the woman I am to portray. I whisper her words and imagine her thoughts. Illuminated, she comes alive in the red room where I sit. Her face is one I saw once while waiting for a traffic light to change. A pale, sad face behind a window, the portrait of a lost life that vanished in a passing car.

While sitting at a desk translating Ibsen's drama, I am overwhelmed by the magic and the possibilities of my profession.

Reading a drama that is a hundred years old, written in rage and anguish, I look forward to rehearsals.

I hope we will establish such tenderness between the mother and her son that when she loses him and all is over, the audience is left shattered by her compassionate fight and defeat.

Hearing his wish to die, she embraces him like a burning lover. She is like a river running full.

The tensile strength of those who challenge destiny: a mother daring the gods to save her child.

And then the ghosts are at her like a plague. She drowns. Death invades the room.

Ibsen writes that she screams. Oh, yes. It is such pain, pulsating as blood drains the body. Now ebb forever.

The scream is an almost soundless gasp.

Day I of rehearsal. Everybody meets for the first reading of the play. For the first time I worry about interpreting Mrs. Alving. All she seems to do is react to the other characters. Will the different actors present me with the crucial elements against which to react?

The director is youthful and very enthusiastic. He doesn't say what he believes the play is about, or what the characters hope for and fear, though he asks us to write down our own thoughts on this.

DAY 2. The director doesn't want us to use the script. Instead we'll improvise scenes. I don't know in what way our improvisations relate to the play. I have fun, though.

DAY 3. We're still not working with Ibsen's words, and we've yet to hear the director's overall concept of the play. There is a very nice and warm atmosphere, however, and we end the day with champagne.

DAY 4. Today we exchange parts: I play Pastor Manders, he plays Mrs. Alving, and so forth. Still no Ibsen. When will I be allowed to use the script? After a while, having laughed at John Neville doing Mrs. Alving and me making a farce of the Pastor, we tire and start discussing the Falklands crisis. Later, we discuss our astrological signs. It turns out that most of the people connected with this production are Taurus. Then we improvise some more: I am told to pretend that I come home to my husband, who has found out that I've been unfaithful for ten years.

There is no husband in *Ghosts*—but the director thinks it might be interesting to see John play one. He really tries very hard to do our improvisation truthfully, and finally starts to cry. When he cries, he reminds me of the scientist I loved. This makes me sad and I feel alienated, because my thoughts wander back into my private past. I don't know what all this has to do with *Ghosts*, since it is never put into perspective with the play.

D A Y   5 .   For the first time, we are allowed to use the script, but are told to concentrate on *one* feeling only. I am asked to play on hate and use "my own hate as a mother." I do not remember hating my child. Exploring something within one's self might be fine, but I don't know if it will benefit the finished production. Hate hardly fits the words Ibsen has written to express Mrs. Alving's sentiments for her son. The director tells me not to worry.

D A Y   6 .   Today we start working with Act II, although there has been no blocking of Act I. We aren't going to block Act II either. We sit around the table reading scenes aloud. I don't want to play only on Mrs. Alving's imaginary hate anymore, and I ask the director if I can have some humiliation and sorrow beneath the hate. "If you'd like to," he says. Somebody sends out for raw fish for lunch.

D A Y   7 .   We concentrate on the scene between Manders and Engstrand in Act II. Mrs. Alving has no lines here and, since we don't do blocking, I have no action either. I'm afraid there's going to be very little time in which to explore why these people move and how they move. Raquel Welch is rehearsing a musical on the same floor as we are on. She comes in to visit. Everyone welcomes the break and we exchange jokes with her until it's time for lunch.

I'm more and more worried that we have no blocking done, nor have we discussed the concept of the play, and most of the time we improvise everything. I feel as if nothing real is happening. I suddenly have the sensation that we're all part of a group of young reconnaissance scouts. I wish I were someplace else. Inside of me, pictures from Ethiopia—from Thailand. Reality is somewhere else—far from this room in which I'm locked all day.

D A Y 8 . Pastor Manders is off in Canada to finish a film. We sit down and read Act II without him, an act in which he is a dominant person. Why can't we work on the scenes between my son and me? The man who plays Osvald is young and has never acted on a big stage.

We discuss the English translation of "Livsglede." The script says "passion and life." But "joy of life" is closer to what Ibsen meant, and we change it.

Very little is done today; mostly we correct the text. When, *finally*, we do work on a scene between my son and me, we *sit*, since we still have no blocking. I am asked to play as if I love him, then do the same scene as if I do *not* love him. I wish we would rehearse the *play*.

D A Y 9 . We are still with Act II. Manders is back. For the first time the director works on blocking. Since he has none prepared, he moves us around to see what it looks like: move here, move there. I feel very uncomfortable. The blocking that evolves doesn't seem to connect with what we're saying, and the characters never move in response to the logic of a situation. I ask the director if I can't stand still until it's clear *why* she walks. He says, "Listen, I'm famous for my movements." I don't know how to answer that.

DAY 10. Osvald and I are told to play our long emotional scene in Act II on the one note that he hates me. I am to have no emotion.

After he has hated me for a while, I get furious. I scowl at the director while my son receives my rage.

A mountain is growing higher and higher in front of us. I don't know how I'm going to go through with this.

DAY 11. The stage manager, his assistant, and the other actors are sitting watching the different blocking improvisations. This makes the director uncomfortable and he brings my son and me into an alcove off the big rehearsal room. There we sit down with our scripts and read to each other.

DAY 12. This will be the final entry in my little notebook on the rehearsals of *Ghosts*.

We are doing Ibsen, who has so many layers to explore, and on day 12 of our twenty-one days of rehearsal without an audience, we still haven't started the blocking of Act II. Act III we just read through once on our first day together.

Goodbye, Mrs. Alving. Goodbye, sweet dreams.

.   .   .

I have spent years and years as an actress playing the game of others. Allowing directors and producers and other actors to set the rules and barriers in the development of our joint production. Whereas I increasingly manage in life to demand the freedom of choice, I tend most often to pick a subordinate role in my profession.

When I sometimes did protest and ask for changes, I was never good at it, or at least not listened to. Always eager to please, I accepted someone else's argument too easily.

You need strength to do it your way, since failure may result from a wrong choice. You need a pride that will not be hurt when someone says you are wrong or when you actually are.

Wisdom decrees that I should try again and again throughout my development to find the truth in my innermost feelings, until I am able to act upon my own preferences.

When we finally open with *Ghosts*, one critic compares my strength and light on stage to that of the sun and the moon. Another writes that the surprising news of his day is that I cannot act at all.

On a talk show during the *Ghosts* run, I'm asked if I can speak one of the well-known lines from the play, just to give the television viewers a little taste.

I want to oblige the interviewer, whom I like, but I have to refuse. I can only do my lines on stage. I'm not a puppet. I have no motive for proving that I can give reality to a faked emotion at any place and time. It feels like selling one's soul, and cheaply.

I saw a famous actress on "60 Minutes." "Cry," they told her. And she did. Big tears rolled down her cheeks. I will never believe in her sincerity again.

Dick Cavett once said to me, "You are an actress. Tell me you love me in a way that I believe it." Of course I could say "I love you" to Dick Cavett if I did love him, but I didn't want to sit on a television program and be phony just to show I can act. That has nothing to do with acting.

I would be like a magician left with an empty hat, trying to lift something out of it. To satisfy an audience.

In acting I am dealing with something extremely fragile. Something unspoken inside myself, and explaining it is almost impossible. The goal, too, is the impossible. It is the cloth weaving the cloth. It is the character creating the character.

The Japanese used to make a special plate for oil which had a lovely design and yet was very inexpensive. The pattern was just a willow tree made by a few soft strokes of pigment to form the decoration. Because these plates cost almost nothing, children were used to paint the design. The great potters today say that adults couldn't paint like that. They wouldn't have the *innocence* to form a tree with just two lines because the soul is no longer pure.

I don't know how one gets back to a pure soul. Yet interpretation must come from an untainted spirit. It is the center of gravity. This bears out the difficulty.

I can never peel off what I am inside—all the contradictions, all the fear and broken dreams and hopes that envelop my core. All the choices I failed to make. All the conflicting facets, colors, pains, and happiness—which are me.

Though somehow the starting point has to come from a center very close to that of a child who can make a willow tree with two lines.

. . .

If the truth of acting really belongs to the discovery of the soul of another human being, can I ever find it? Because whose hearts and souls can be captured?

The pleasure comes from watching the performer who, with a single movement of his head, explains everything.

If I do not always keep doing things, the audience is allowed to *recognize* through me what *they* believe in. They should participate with their own experience. Be creators. Enter with their own fantasy.

The difficulty with the simplicity of a perfect gesture or inflection is that it is not simple. Yet everything goes to pieces when the purity is lost.

I recall the moment when I created laughter the day before, and in wishing to hear it again, I exaggerate the moment—and lose it.

Once the audience has given me the gift of its positive reaction, I have lost my innocence. Since innocence is born of spontaneity, it is difficult to reproduce.

My unconscious is the real creator.
The body has a wisdom of its own.
Charlie Parker once told a saxophonist, "Don't play it, let it play you."
I must let the instrument, which is my character, play me.

. . .

Each actor has to create his own images.

Our material is the life we are living and the life we are seeing, the life we are reading and the life we are listening to.

But never to use present *personal* emotions, never private anger or private grief, because what my passions fail to do themselves, everything I *know* about passion accomplishes.

The truth of acting for me is to open myself in such a way that the character is allowed to appear through me. If the character needs to cry, it is the character who does it, not I. It is Liv uncovered, permitting myself to stand on the side and watch. It is like having an instrument so tuned that whatever you choose to play on it will come out truthfully. In golden moments that can happen. I believe that the challenge of acting is to find that truth.

In a strange way, as I grow older, although there is an ever increasing inventory of experience, I find that what I want to bring to acting is ever simpler and purer. I wish I could return one day to the moment when I knew how to paint a willow tree with just two strokes.

In almost my favorite comment on acting, Yeats wrote of the Noh drama: "A young man was following a stately old woman through the streets of a Japanese town, and presently she turned to him and spoke: 'Why do you follow me?'

" 'Because you are so interesting.'

" 'That is not so, I am too old to be interesting.' But he wishes, he told her, to become a player of old women on the Noh stage. If he would become famous as a Noh player, she said, he must not observe life, nor put on an old face and stint the music of his voice. He must know how to suggest an old woman and yet find it all in his heart."

Millions of years ago we emerged from the water and crawled ashore. On the dry land we are still seeking our purpose, just as some primal urge made us choose to leave the sea for the land.

During our short time on earth, we exercise and follow choices, with all their ambiguities. We learn that little is clear-cut, life's most difficult choices can seem indistinct. The most profound aspirations have costs as well as benefits.

Absolute good and evil may not exist.

A long time ago I played in Brecht's *Caucasian Chalk Circle*. My name was Grusha.

I am sitting beside a baby whose mother has abandoned it. I am very poor and very frightened. As I bend down to pick up the child, wrapped in silk and velvet, precious materials I have never touched before, I am filled with doubts. The child will be a hindrance in my life. I barely have food and clothing for myself. I walk away.

But then I stop. I return. Reluctantly, I sit down close to the infant again. I look at it, then look away.

Finally, I pick it up. Rebuke it for the difficulties I will now be faced with. Laugh to it because it is so pitiful and helpless.

I am the one who passed by and was able to help.

· · ·

D R O U G H T . In the middle of a dry landscape in Latin America, I see a small vegetable garden, seedlings twisted around thin sticks dug into the dry earth for support. A scent of wildflowers drifts across to me. An old lady tends this garden, which is not her own. She wears a loose-fitting dress, and a tiny straw hat balances on top of her head while she points with pride to the different rows of green. Under the almost colorless shapes of leaves she is showing me, I detect tomatoes and beans.

"Only the smallest children in our village will eat these vegetables. There isn't enough for all. That is why I am asked to guard the garden."

There is pride in her voice: near the end of her life, people in the community have demonstrated their trust in her. Night and day she stays with her responsibility. Two small trees, of which the stem of one is burned black by sun, droop like death over her shack, which is placed by the entrance to the vegetable yard.

She holds one arm up toward me, dry and withered like everything around her, and says, "I get almost no water. What we have goes mostly for this garden. My life is to guard these vegetables that I will never eat."

F L O O D . On the coast of Ecuador there are heavy rains that the rivers cannot absorb. The water is backing up and spilling over the poor communities. The streets are filled with thick, green water, which is dangerous playing ground for children. Balancing on primitive bridges between the huts made out of bamboo and wood—sometimes with heavy loads on their backs—the children fall off and drown, since few of them can swim.

There is no electricity, very few latrines, no food, drinking water is a long journey away—and as usual, more expensive for the poor than for the well off.

"We need so many things."

The woman's hands are in constant movement, stroking her dress, her hair, clasping the palms together before she wipes a tear from eyes that never, never look up from the floor that is already ankle-deep in water.

"We need so much, especially for our children. They need a space to run. There are some fields and green places in the big city, but it is too far away for them to walk. Here we have only water. And it is rising all the time."

EARTHQUAKE.   He is in his late sixties. His home is gone. He is sharing a tent with his neighbors.

"I was leaving my house to go to work at the time the earthquake happened. I had walked half a block when I saw that all the cables and telegraph poles were shaking. I turned to my house hoping these movements would go back to normal again, and I saw the road—it was like waves. I tried to walk and I fell down. I saw everything around me falling down and I wondered if I would survive. I was frozen. I was paralyzed. I got to my house and as I was entering I saw my neighbor's home tumbling to the ground. Dust was coming off the cement and everywhere houses were breaking down and the whole atmosphere was becoming dust. There was no fire. I got into my house and I was terrified. I didn't want to go out anymore.

"At noon somebody came to pick me up, to help in the

emergency. I was very scared as I left my home. All these walls that used to protect me—they were all falling.

"Now I hope someone will tell me what to do. I am just waiting."

Popayán was, before the earthquake, a very traditional city, a sanctuary. It was the birthplace of presidents and poets, and Colombians were proud of its history and the monuments and churches of colonial times.

Everywhere people are sitting along the destroyed streets, just watching. Some big construction machines are already starting to push away demolished houses. There is a sense of disaster all around.

More than three thousand graves were opened by the earthquake, and the bodies came shooting out. Some corpses flew considerable distances. One woman was rumored to have gone mad when a corpse chased her down a hill. A reporter commented: "I don't need to see any more Hitchcock films—they are here."

With the earthquake, well-hidden poverty appeared, like the corpses. It is as if the earthquake shook the poverty out.

A little boy draws a house for me. It has a small garden and is beautifully decorated with flowers and plants. He tells me this is his home, although we are sitting in mud surrounded by his mother's casseroles and a few sticks she is saving for fuel.

The fact of their life is that they have no money, no means to obtain work. They cannot get a loan because they would probably be unable to pay it back. Like many thousands of others, they are living on private property they have invaded. There is no water system and no system for garbage and sanitation. It seems unbearable in the heavy winds and constant rain to live as most do here—without roofs.

The house the little boy draws has curtains in the windows and pine trees around.

Many people I meet see the earthquake as the result of a curse made by a famous Colombian general, who said: "When the cross of the old church made of stone falls down, I wish the city to be destroyed. And it will happen on a Holy Thursday."

This was the prophecy, and it came true on Holy Thursday in 1983. Now, a few days later, I watch people go to the place with the cross, where they kneel and ask forgiveness.

The old man who had lost his house tells me what a quiet city Popayán used to be. "Our city commemorated dedication and Jesus Christ and silence. It was beautiful, all robes and ornaments and colors."

We are sitting in his tent and its thin walls don't keep out the rain. The old man is shivering:

"Holy Week in Popayán is the most important week of the year because many tourists come and there are concerts. Famous orchestras and choirs traveled to Popayán to commemorate the death of Christ. But we became too dependent on the tourists and became pagans and heretics because we were having parties instead of suffering in memory of the death of Christ. In Popayán there was more drinking

during Holy Week than at any other time during the year.
God decided to do this, as He did to Sodom and Gomorrah."

It has been raining hard for three days, and the homeless
and the poor huddle in the rubble of the streets or in make-
shift shelters.

A young woman feels so hopeless describing her situation that she sinks down into the mud and sobs quietly. Her
thin arms are crossed in front of her face. Faintly, I hear
the sounds of grief.

There are walls along the streets of Manila most frequented by tourists. Behind the walls is poverty.

SHELTER. Her home is two square meters of cardboard laid out on the pavement. In her lap, a child is resting. The mother is sitting with her legs stretched out in front of her—an image of solitude untouched by the sounds of the city and the bustling crowds and traffic of the streets. The parks and rivers and bridges and grand mansions are not part of her hidden life.

Her child is sleeping and she has closed her eyes while guarding the center of her life with her soft, bent body.

COMPASSION. He looks like a wounded animal, surveying the poor community before him. His long face shines with sweat. A sad young doctor in torn Levi's, who visits every day.

"I have insufficient medicine and vitamins. I have no serum for immunization."

He halts when a little child approaches him and he lifts her up—both of them are laughing. The moment she wiggles out of his arms and runs away, he returns to his solemn attitude.

"I come here because they are so deprived, but really I am helpless to treat them."

Surrounding us are shacks with black and gray tin roofs.

He points to the sewage that runs in brown streams along the narrow path where we walk. "It takes a strong child to survive surrounded by poison."

I ask why he doesn't stay with his private practice in the prosperous part of Manila.

"I come," he says, "to be here and help God perform a miracle."

M I L K . In the only community shop, half of the shelves are filled with milk formula for infants. It is promoted extensively through radio, television, newspapers, and even by many doctors. Behind the walls of Manila, I meet few mothers who breastfeed their babies. Great carnage is being caused by those who manufacture this product and promote it for use by poor women: there is only contaminated water available to mix with the powder—and fuel to boil it is almost nonexistent. The cost of a can is about fifty pesos, much more than one day's wages in most families.

Breast milk, on the other hand, is a nutritious stream, rich in immunological agents for the infants. And it is free.

In the midst of mothers holding weak, malnourished babies, I see a woman rocking a fat little boy in her arms. He is sleeping so contentedly—with rosy cheeks—and I know before I ask her what she will answer.

"Do you breastfeed your child?"

"Yes."

This three-month-old baby—bigger than most two-year-olds here—is brought by his mother to the square where UNICEF has arranged a meeting for the women of the community. Still sleeping as if he is drunk from milk, the boy becomes a living illustration to mothers whose infants have

perished that they have been cheated by immoral pro-
motion.

Fat Rexus—that is his royal name—has gained a victory
for all of them against those who coax women into disastrous
dependence on powdered milk mixed with dirty water.

Three-month-old Rexus is one of the true third-world
success stories, although he will never make any headlines.

Y O U T H . She is dancing along the road. There is a
rigid discipline to her steps: one foot high—then a little
skip—put the one foot down so the other one can kick up
high. Her soul is dancing too, freer than her bare feet.
When she rests her feet for a moment, soul still moving
happily, she tells me she is one hundred and fifteen years
old.

"One hundred and fifteen years old?"

"Yes. And you can tell I am old only because I have a
weak knee and weak hips."

Liar that she is! There seems to be nothing weak about
her jumping back and forth, though just now when she
stands still I see that her body is, in fact, quite twisted. Then
up and around she goes again.

"You have had a long life," I shout after her.

"I am still here because I have strong faith in God." A
little pause in front of me. "Once I had cancer and they
told me I had only fifteen more years to live. That was a
long time ago. Lately, I have been looking around to get
married!"

She starts dancing again.

"My husband died during the Japanese time." Shrieks
of laughter. She is a little out of breath now, as it's getting

hard to make conversation while kicking first one foot up in the air and then the other.

"I go around searching for a man and my legs get shorter and shorter."

"What should he look like?"

"Very old. There is life and wisdom in an old one. I'll find one for you, too."

She whispers to me confidentially, her legs momentarily still. "I lied about my age. I'm really only one hundred and six."

Teaching. I am being driven to one of the poor communities seated on the heights above the city. The saying goes: "The poor have the best view in Colombia."

I look at the nests clustered on the telephone wires we're driving past. Close together, black dots looking like my grandmother's balls of wool. I wonder if the birds listen to our conversation when we phone. Are they kept warm by our voices floating on the wires?

At the school where I am taken I meet a tall, handsome man with a beautiful smile that lights up a gentle face.

The children in his school, which has no roof and only two walls, are guided through a program of engineering and agriculture. His aim is to make them managers of their own community.

They are shown how to garden and to identify plants with medicinal properties. Around the ground are scattered bee colonies, for which the children have all the responsibility.

Parents, welcoming the possibilities of education given to their children, decided to build a road to the schoolhouse in order to make it more accessible for those who lived far away. Today the road penetrates an area of former wilderness.

Because of contaminated water, pollution-related illnesses used to be a major problem. The teacher started to treat the school water with filters and chemicals and passed the information on to his pupils. After learning these methods, the children brought the new knowledge back to their homes.

Today this school is visited by community leaders of distant regions, who study his program.

"I look upon my work as a portrait of what I can do in life."

He tells me that he had been a lawyer but decided to become a monk. But while he was on his way to the monastery, many people from his poor area followed him along the road pleading for his help, since he was the only educated man among them. So he stayed.

He owns a cow. It is solemnly contemplating the possibilities of a fenced-in vegetable garden.

"One day we shall have a school cafeteria from this garden."

We stroll on to a fish pond of which he is very proud. It is artificial, one and a half meters deep, ten meters long, five meters wide. The fish are fed with salad leaves, and I watch the leaves move as the fish eat from beneath. In the end, only the veins are left floating on the water.

People in the area can afford to eat meat only occasionally and fish used to be unknown. No longer.

Again this smile that lights up his whole face.

"I really wanted to be a monk, but sometimes you are asked to serve in a different way.

"You are asked to plant without knowing the use of it. But you are the only one who can do it."

Story. A nun showing me the beauties of the church she serves points to a tiny window—the only one—high up on the wall.

"A long time ago a monk was assisting here—famous for his gentleness and compassion. But in the night his body grew hot and he went to the crucifix there—using it as his ladder, employing Jesus' shoulder to climb through the window. Each time Jesus would ask him, 'How long are you going to keep this up?'

" 'Till I am back,' the monk would say, 'when the night is over.' One day, as he was sneaking out, he happened to be caught in the middle of a funeral procession and he asked, 'Who are you burying?'

" 'Father Leonard.'

"Since this was his name, he quietly climbed back again, using Jesus' shoulder as his ladder for the last time. Repenting, he closed himself in for nine years and when he finally emerged, the people elected him the holy patron of the church."

The nun points again to the wall. "As you can see, we now have his statue in the window over the crucifix of Jesus." She blinks her eye at me and laughs for a long time, thinking of her brother.

CHILDHOOD. I spent a night with some of the many thousand street children in Colombia. They are small and so feisty. Full of fantasy and eager suggestions for where we should go together now that we have been introduced. What about some restaurant? We eat chicken and chips in a dingy little place, and every time their small fingers grab a piece of food, it is first offered to me.

Dirty little hands rest on my lap and one or another arm is always around my waist. A child of six or seven drops his head on my shoulder, pretending to fall asleep leaning his frail body close to mine. Small boys and I laugh and kiss and touch, we share no other language. Do not need to.

When they finally tire, they ask if I'll take them home. We locate the cardboard sheet they have hidden. Outside a jewelry shop their pavement is still vacant. Their blanket is the sack they dragged along all night and with gestures they demand that I tuck them in.

This is when these small children's arms are lifted toward me; tough little street children become vulnerable, abandoned boys. Wanting to be kissed good night.

For just a moment I lie down with them. They let me hold them—close. I feel their warm breath, I stroke their foreheads, hold their hands, allowing them to snuggle against the body of the mother they are missing.

In this sweep of time, I am no longer homesick for my childhood. Suddenly, at home in their trust, I know what I have been looking for, why I have traveled.

I am *me*.

I open the door to Linn's room carefully. She is sleeping. Her head is turned toward the window—she has forgotten to draw the curtain. Sun creates light and shadow on her face. I kiss her. From under her covers two small heads appear—a white, furry one with big, surprised eyes, and an aristocratic yellow-brown one with green, arrogant eyes: her cats.

They are forbidden to enter her bed but wait patiently each night until she is asleep before they invade the privacy of her big Norwegian eiderdown.

Since I am usually a likely food provider, they leave their present haven, both of them purring—one of them smiling —while they look admiringly and lovingly at me.

Being an easy target for flattery, I leave them only after providing canned sardines in tomato sauce from Norway. (A special favorite of mine that my mother sends me now and then.)

The cats don't even acknowledge my departure. Two tails in slow and indolent movements, bottoms turned to me as they empty their plates with pink little tongues. I have served my purpose.

It is a beautiful Sunday morning in May. Time for rebirth as nature's flood tide rises again and overflows the ground with growth.

Birds are singing; thrush and titmouse and wagtail and swallow and cuckoo, all of them outside her window. And not far away I listen to a brook of melted snow run down the mountainside.

All the lovely light colors of spring surrounding us. A little farther down from our house, old Miss Gran will soon be out digging in her tiny garden: she will wear a blue dress and a blue hat, coloring the spring herself—not the least through her joy of meeting it all again.

Abel and I sit on the cliff looking at our fjord. For once it is quiet. A large ship is on its way to cross the ocean.

I remember an ocean and another man who, on the island we shared, predicted, "You and I are painfully connected."

As if Abel reads my thoughts, he asks, "Do you want me to tell you about your island?"

Around me I feel spring, I feel the tides turn. And I close my eyes while I tell him to describe the island for me, as if I had never talked to him about it.

Slowly, he says, "I see a beautiful princess in captivity. I see her loneliness, see her fear, her struggle with the master of the island. I see the island as an isolated, experimental love shelter."

I shake my head. "You are a real child, Abel. You don't understand."

This doesn't faze him.

"I like fairy tales. You told me that after the island, nothing could hurt you anymore. I thought that something terrible had happened to you to make you invulnerable. I thought that something in you had died forever. Then I understood what you wanted to tell me."

"Sweet Abel. You think you understand."

"You asked me never to forget your wound," he murmurs into my hair. "Your enormous, incurable wound."

"I asked you to look at the proof that I had been living while you were reading," I think as I gently watch him.

Dearest Abel. I am not a princess out of a fairy tale. I am a woman whose journey took her to an island for a time in her life.

You would like to hear a story about an unhappy woman who went out of her mind, who was seen at night on the beach, still beautiful, standing motionless and staring eternally into the sea.

So that it would all be definite.

He is silent. We are resting, wrapped around each other on top of a cliff on a spring afternoon before anyone else has moved into the surrounding summer houses.

Then he says, and again he seems to read my thoughts, "I would truly like that."

"You would truly like what?" I ask.

"I would like you to surprise me," he answers. "I would like you to come to me defeated, like anyone else. The idea of not being able to cry over you drives me wild."

Suddenly the sun is no longer warm. Summer is far away. "Should I feel defeated because I love you?"

He says, "You should feel defeated because you've loved many times."

PART FOUR

PARTING

Saying goodbye to a part. I have been so close to a character whom I am never going to meet again. It is the character for the last time. Everything she meant to me. Now it is time to leave.

These tears of farewell are not mine. It is the role crying, knowing she will never exist again.

I have always lived close to water.

Water brought me to my different homes. The oceans have been roads to new epochs of my life.

Water gave me peace when I sat watching its surface.

The surface is tidal, but underneath is that which never moves, the everlasting deep.

I feel the ebbs and the flows within me—as well as that which is unmovable in the sea.

A woman contains the ocean from which man is born. Man leaves this ocean on the first day of his life and is on a journey away from it until the end.

Woman stays with her beginning.

Man is an island, but woman is her own ocean in which her island rests.

The distance between man and woman comes in part from these different frames of reference.

I often feel with Abel now that I disturb the life he wants for himself. I feel I disrupt his chance for harmony and creativity.

I want it to be over. But I never know how to leave. And when someone leaves me, I panic and mourn the parting as if death has come between us.

But we are living together like strangers, and we seem to destroy every action and word of the other.

Sometimes I believe the reason I cling to this destructive relationship so stubbornly is because I know that, once he has gone, I will be forced to deal with pain. Alone.

He is sitting in the bedroom by the window. He does not turn to look at me when I enter. I can sense he has been drinking. His hair is still wet, he must have showered—maybe just got up from bed, although it's already late afternoon. He talks—addressing the window, the skyscrapers, and everything else on the other side of the glass, the cold gray air, the sounds and the frenzy that belong to New York. Everything my bedroom windows cannot protect him from. His neck is vulnerable. I want to touch it. Instead I lie down on the bed and listen.

"My travels used to give me so much, until one day the process reversed itself. I realized that there was a taking away. That's why I want to settle down, stay in one place, a place where I belong. I don't belong here in your blue room. I don't want to walk with a cane because I live in New York where I can't work. I'm frightened of turning into stone. I see that the frontiers are open. I just don't want to cross them anymore."

He turns his handsome face toward me. Because he's been drinking, I don't really exist for him—his words are part of a personal monologue. He does not want answers, feedback. He doesn't even want me as a listener. He just needs my presence, like the view from my bedroom window. His anger and his frustration have to be directed toward something, have to include everything he feels is suffocating him. And while he encloses me with darkness and sorrow, he drags me into his misery and I fear I shall drown as well. He looks through me and lifts a glass to his mouth and whispers, "I am incapable of doing what I haven't done before, what life hasn't already confirmed. That is why I can't accept new beliefs and new experiences. When I told you, 'Use me'—I meant something simple. I wanted to be *me* with *you*. *Be.* The purpose of life is just that: to *be* there and disappear. For me there is no other purpose."

He drinks. He covers his face in his hands. I love him. But I do not move, just lie silently on the bed.

"I believe in love," he is still whispering. "I dream about it. But it has to be overwhelming. It has to make me soar. If it's not like that—it's only another platitude. I loved you, but you didn't allow me to soar."

He takes his hands away. If I turned my head I would see his face. Maybe I could reach him if he saw in my eyes that I knew what he was saying.

"But when you didn't understand my reason for being here with you, when you didn't know enough to join me in the adventure which was you and me, you castrated me."

He starts crying. I leave the room.

I go into the living room. I start pulling out different books, looking through one, then another. And then I give up and bend my head over my knees.

He is standing in the door. Looking at his hands as if seeing them for the first time.

"I wanted to lose the past but I couldn't," he says to me. "I live the past. The past doesn't change."

He leaves the apartment. I hear the door bang and I know he will be late and very drunk. I try to catch a glimpse of him from the window.

Hanging alongside the window frame are family pictures. In photographs we will eventually all line up for posterity.

Staring out into space, never to exist again that way. Pictures measuring all that we were with time.

I touch a photograph, then follow the lines on my face with my finger. I leave the apartment.

On the streets of New York, dusk is creeping around the buildings and the people and the cars and the dirt. I am aware of the surroundings, the sounds, the scents, and in the end, curiously, comforted by all that is known and familiar.

A sudden childhood memory from Norway. I am swimming.

Gliding through the dark of night. Naked.

Before me, the pale light from a full moon makes a luminescent avenue without end on the water.

Around me phosphorescence of the sea. Animals of the sea.

Thousands of diamonds approach me, and when I flow through them, they escape in all directions. Leaving me awed by their shimmering trails, me, the young girl.

In the midst of the black and gray skyscrapers of New York, I see the endless concrete surrounding me, and know that there is still magic in a fjord of Norway.

It is the end of the night. We are sitting together. I hold him. He talks. Gently, I stroke his hair, kiss his neck. I let him know by small touches and whispers of understanding that I'm listening. He doesn't respond to me. He is lost in his own agonizing world. I know we have to leave each other.

He confesses to the night, unaware that I am close and want to help.

"Alone with you I can't cope. I say the wrong things. I hardly touch you except when we're in bed. But when we're with others, I want to hold you all the time. I keep caressing you for everyone to see." He weeps.

"A man is a public animal. He does in public what he can't do in privacy—he's shy when he's alone. Masculinity is a public affair. It's for showing off. The crowd is his god. Animalism is his nature. He's fighting for recognition from the other animals."

It's as if I'm sitting in a corner watching him with me—performing a role. And, as if in a film, the dialogue is acted out.

. . .

SHE: I don't have time anymore to be your mother or your child. I don't have time anymore to let you decide for me whether this will be a good day or a bad one. I don't have time anymore to be defined by you.

HE: You're afraid of wasting time?

SHE: There's a young girl in me who will not die. She tells me there's so much out there that I was never close to. I want to investigate it all. I want to have roots in nothing but myself. And, yes, I want to love.

I don't want love with you, because it's dependency.

I want to break my pattern, and while I do, I'll acknowledge the hurt and the loneliness as unavoidable and a part of my life.

HE: You are telling me to leave?

SHE: I am telling you that you were never really here. We thought we loved each other—but we loved our dreams of the past and our hopes for the future.

HE: At this moment—here and now—I know I love you.

SHE: At this moment—here and now—I know I love you, too. Because of the sun coming in through the window. Because of the color of your sweater—because of your lovely chest and your strong arms. At this moment I love you, too, because your eyes are unhappy—because of my memory of your mouth, of your body. I love you because your soul is sweet and I love you because you're intelligent. Because you touched me so much, and made me laugh. But that isn't enough.

HE: You talk like a child, and I want to understand you. I don't want to leave you—because you can't be alone. You'll be hurt and you'll be isolated. You're no longer

young, and those who want you now might want you for
the wrong reasons. I'll marry you, and I'll help you when
you need help.

You're anxious and you're dissatisfied. You're also disappointed. You need a man to protect you. You need me.
Don't turn me away. I might be your last chance. Maybe
you can still have a baby—then you won't have to travel
the world to satisfy your need to mother.

SHE: I leave you because you don't recognize me. I leave
you because I don't want to try anymore to be everything
that I'm not. I leave you because I'm going to be *me* and
live my life the way I believe in it. I leave you because I'm
the one who's responsible for what I feel and know and
understand.

And I'll miss you—I'll miss the warmth of your embrace
and the knowledge of someone being there when I come
home, and I'll miss you for all the wrong reasons. Probably
I'll cry and ask you to come back. But don't come. You are
no longer to be a refuge, my reason for self-esteem and my
pride.

HE: You once said, "Nothing can hurt me anymore." Do you
know that you're moving toward a lot of hurt?

SHE: Yes. But that's not a reason for us to stay together.
Fear is a prison from which love can never emerge. (*He
gets up from the bed and sits in a chair. He looks at her a
long time.*)

HE: You are in flight from your past life.

SHE: I am homesick for my past—but at the same time I
want to open my life to more and more things. I don't want
the same repertoire all my life.

I want to reevaluate my work. I don't only want an audi-

ence. I want what I do to *matter*. I want to *deserve* survival.
HE: Before I met you, I was ill. I didn't want people. I didn't want to relate. I didn't even want to listen to myself anymore. I was forty years old and I was prepared to sit down and wait for death, accompanied by my books and my music. *You* didn't change that. But the frustration I felt, the anger I often perceived about you—watching you run around trying to find your mission in life—it left me looking at my own illness, facing my own death—and then I didn't die, I survived. I'm in a remission. I'm not canceling my experience with you—my view of life has changed. But because I've been so close to destruction, I can never be what you would like me to be.

If you are leaving me, I'll go on with my life. Sometimes I'll think of you, but I am not sure I'll miss you.
SHE: I will be the one to miss.
HE: I love you.
SHE: I'm not sure I know how to love, but in my imperfect way, I love you, too.
HE: Hold me. (*She goes over to him, puts her arms around him. They stay like that for a long time. Then he moves away from her. Looks at her for a moment. He goes. She watches the door close behind him. Cut.*)

She is on a voyage of solitude. Her need is for space.

No more words and no more music come alive in her, though *she* can live through certain writing and certain tunes.

She is no more and no less than the way her face glows or doesn't glow. She is the way she listens or doesn't listen. She is the sentences uttered by her coming alive or dying.

She is on a voyage of solitude, feeling close to something, though it isn't to the man resting at her side that she feels close. It isn't his arm holding her tight while he's still asleep or the way he sighs and turns. It is not he.

They met and they talked together and they learned something from each other. But when her senses reminded her of the power of being alone, when she felt that she was losing something in losing solitude—she started to withdraw. She slept with him and was still alone in the quietness of their room, in the light of a lamp during his embraces.

She had hoped to visit an enchanted garden, a haven, without looking back—but in the end she found herself on a renewed voyage of solitude.

Her bed is the earth, and she closes her eyes, feeling safe under the blankets and against the pillow on which her head lies.

The pressure of his arm around her body is something she forgets when she starts sinking into a dream while still awake.

Her eyelids are closed over an ever present blue stare.

In the beginning the movement is slow, and because her eyes are closed it is hard to know whether she is just imagining wind on her cheeks. The blanket almost covers her head, and then—during the dark—it happens. The dark is no longer black—silver streaks and golden pearls and red shining glass join her, flashing past.

The beauty of her voyage—silver and gold and sparkling crystal.

Rainbows and soft whispers and moist kisses.

The pearls she captures, she captures them in her warm hand and feels how they live and make movements in the inside of her palm. Promising riches if she ever reaches her destiny, which is the sunshine—which is solitude.

And now she can sense how she is flying, flying over a sea—a blue ocean—now a black ocean—a mirror of green, of gray. She cannot tell what color the water is.

And the wind lifts the blankets of her bed—and her outstretched arms are sails. No wings. How wonderfully freely her white arms allow her to glide, to fall, to rise.

Thus, as she whirls and turns and soars over the sea with all its colors and white foam—solitude invades her body, emptying it of everything and everyone.

A sense of power from being alone. Alone. Alone.

The power of being alone with oceans and winds.

In this power of solitude—she leaves the safety of the arm holding her body, the strong profile on the pillow beside her. And she whirls around the earth where she can no longer feel the energy of the ground, where she can no longer see the grass and the trees and everything she knows.

She is the sound around her, the wind itself. When she finally pierces the ocean, falls and falls through the water, she passes everything familiar without recognition. She is the Deep itself.

I say his lies for him, to ease my hurt.

I tell him: "Call me when you like." I never mention yearning.

I almost cannot breathe. They call it lack of oxygen.

I know that it is lack of love.

I feel sometimes just like a fisherman who was granted three wishes by the grateful genie. Like him I want the two I made first to be undone.

I wished: "Oh, let him see me."

And then I wished: "Let us be lovers."

Now I want them both undone.

I know the meaning of his silence, before he finds the courage to put truth behind his phrases. And when at last he vanishes without a word, I learn the iron rule:

Leave first. Just disappear.

How is it possible? He told me: Dare to fly!

Bullshit.

(And I am six again—when father died—and I was left alone, with no instructions.)

I learn the iron rule: Leave first.

Or else die of love for one who cannot love.

I never had the chance to tell him how I feel:

"Because I love you, I give you trust. Because you let me love you, be the keeper of my love.

"And since you are the keeper, and it has to end—oh— please be careful not to make it hurt too much."

PART FIVE

TIDES

It makes me unhappy to realize that I will be *fortunate* if I never find what I am looking for, since that way I can never stop seeking.

I want to experience the way I was *then*, when I was very young—the sounds and the fragrances, the faces of my childhood. I am looking for the child in myself. The lost innocence. The purity and freedom. Truth. But I find that everything that *was* is gone forever.

It may be unrealistic to try and get back what one was, though one way or another this is a journey we all make when we start feeling our mortality.

The child within me knew what the adult will never know. For so long I looked at my childhood and wondered if it was really mine. I looked at this person who was me, and looking at her I found myself lost.

The more I learned, the less I understood; the more I remembered, the more lost I felt.

While looking for myself I was fleeing from myself.

I tried to make the ghosts within me speak.

My grandmother, sighing in her bed, unaware of being watched by me, the little girl. Twenty, thirty years later, in a fundamental way, I restore her to life.

She is a sweet lady of Macao, and Mrs. Alving in Ibsen's play. She is Hannah in Auschwitz and a weeping mother in the Philippines. She is you, too, Abel—and I wish I had recognized that while you were still here.

The loudest cry is soundless and stays with us only as our own secret.

Sometimes you were so depressed you would say, without laughing, "I will never be a lucky man. Even if I become famous, no one will know about it. If my suit fell out of the window, I would be inside it."

Oh, Abel.

I had a dream a week ago.

A little girl is crawling in the streets of New Delhi.

Since she is crippled and tired, she has difficulty reaching the pavement she seems to be heading toward. Cars are speeding past her. You lift her up and carry her carefully a long, long time, waiting for a signal to stop, until you understand that she has no direction, she only wants to cross the street. She is laughing in your arms, she lies there like a little queen, taking obvious pleasure in your walk together. Then suddenly she points to a big square in which green grass, trees, and flowers are planted all around to beautify the spot. Love comes through the eyes of this child when she is placed on the soft ground. Through her eyes comes love as if in finding her this haven, you had opened a door to Paradise. Her whole face shines upon you as a sun. She rests under the trees that are all twisted, like herself— eternally cool shadows flowing over her.

She is homeless and despised, yet while looking up at the leaves and the branches and the blue sky, she seems for a moment to be filled with happiness.

I am not out to change the world, I do not even understand *what* will change the world. I only know that some traces of all of us are left behind, although the stages of our journeys are different.

Linn and I walk by the oceanside—the tides are changing.

The wind has colored her cheeks red.

Or is it the wind?

She is quiet—a soft little smile is playing games on her face.

I never saw that smile before.

You grow up by growing apart, my daughter, while I am learning to let go.

Let me tell you a story:

"There was a man who was ninety years old and he was planting a tree. Three young boys passed him and they looked at him and they ran around him and they mocked him. They said to each other, 'I could understand if he was making something with his hands to help the time go by, but to *plant* at his age!'

"The man behaved as if he didn't hear them. Silently, he dug a hole and planted his tree. Not long after, he died.

"Thirty years later, the young boys had turned into middle-aged men and, passing a tree, they took delight in its ripe fruits, which they picked and shared—without recognition."

"How long will you keep telling me stories, Mama?"
"If you will let me—always."
"Will you be lonely when I leave home?"
"No. But I will miss you very much."
"Do you think you'll fall in love again?"
"I know I will."

There is a story I used to hear as a child—of the snow-drop that bloomed in April, hoping to meet the rose, her prince.

"I am waiting for the rose, my suitor, the son of summer. He has set our tryst here. I could not wait, I have come too early; but he will come."

Thus every new spring the snowdrop appeared just after the snow had melted, hoping and waiting in vain.

I used to be like that snowdrop—wondering whether the rose, on hearing my story, would leave its red petals for me as a sign. Until slowly—during the years with Abel—I grew wiser. The more I understood, the more I learned; the more I experienced others, the more I remembered. When people I never knew before touched me with compassion, I did not need to look for myself anymore.

Linn and I walk in silence. It's getting dark. We're heading home. A small blue flower has somehow been uprooted, blown by the wind toward the beach—and now, caught by the tide, is slowly floating away from us.

"It takes a long time to plant a real flower, one that will

last," I say to my child. "We come along with our books and with our papers and with all our measurements, and we try to grow a perfect plant that will bloom forever and give importance to our lives."

I look at her. She still has her smile—and she does not speak.

There is a mother in Ethiopia whose arms are empty now because she lives without choice. I watched her raise a cupped hand filled with polluted water to her starving child.

There is a little girl in Bangladesh who celebrated the installment of a water pump in her village: "I want to show you everything that is wonderful in my life. I want to show you my home, my family, and everything that grows."

There is a young teacher in Colombia whose smile lights up his whole face: "I really wanted to be a monk, but sometimes you are asked to serve in a different way. You are asked to plant without knowing the use of it. But you are the only one who can do it."

There is a woman in Norway who tries to understand.

International Rescue Committee
386 Park Avenue South
New York, N.Y. 10016

Unicef
866 United Nations Plaza
New York, N.Y. 10017

A NOTE ON THE TYPE

The text of this book was set on the Linotype in Fairfield, a typeface designed by the distinguished American artist and engraver Rudolph Ruzicka (1883–1978). Fairfield displays the sober and sane qualities of a master craftsman whose talent has long been dedicated to clarity. Rudolph Ruzicka was born in Bohemia and came to America in 1894. He designed and illustrated many books and was the creator of a considerable list of individual prints in a variety of techniques.

Composed by Maryland Linotype, Inc.
Baltimore, Maryland

Printed and bound by
Fairfield Graphics
Fairfield, Pennsylvania

Designed by Iris Weinstein